WORLD CONFERENCE ON EDUCATION FOR SUSTAINABLE DEVELOPMENT

WORLD CONFERENCE ON EDUCATION FOR SUSTAINABLE DEVELOPMENT

Editor

Dr. Digumarti Bhaskara Rao

M.Sc., M.A., M.A., M.Ed., Ph.D.

Reader & Research Director
RVR College of Education
Guntur-522006, India

&

Member

Board of Studies in Education
Acharya Nagarjuna University
Nagarjuna Nagar-522510

DISCOVERY PUBLISHING HOUSE PVT. LTD.

NEW DELHI-110 002

Published by:
Tilak Wasan

DISCOVERY PUBLISHING HOUSE PVT. LTD.
4383/4A, Ansari Road, Darya Ganj
New Delhi-110 002 (India)
Phone : +91-11-23279245, 43596064-65
Fax : +91-11-23253475
E-mail : parul.wasan@gmail.com
discoverypublishinghouse@gmail.com
web : www.discoverypublishinggroup.com

***First Edition:* 2012**

ISBN: 978-93-5056-018-1

World Conference on Education for Sustainable Development

Printed at:
Shree Balaji Art Press
Delhi

Preface

The *UNESCO World Conference on Education for Sustainable Development—Moving into the Second Half of the* UN *Decade* of Education for Sustainable Development (2005-2014) was held from 31 March to 2 April 2009 in Bonn, Germany. The Organisers of the Conference were the UNESCO and the German Federal Ministry of Education and Research in cooperation with the German Commission for UNESCO.

The Conference objectives were: (1) to highlight the relevance of ESD to all of education; (2) to promote international exchange on ESD, especially between the North and the South; (3) to carry out a stock-taking of the implementation of the UN Decade; and (4) to develop strategies for the way ahead.

The participants of the Conference exchanged the best practices on Education for Sustainable Development from all the regions of the world. They developed mechanisms for enhanced cooperation in the implementation of the UN Decade of Education for Sustainable Development (2005-2014), especially focussing on the exchange between developing countries, those in transition and industrialized countries. Furthermore, the participants discussed regional, national and cultural differences as well as challenges in the implementation of the UN Decade. At the end of the Conference, a Declaration reflecting the debates and proposing guidelines for the implementation of the UN Decade in its second half was adopted.

The book contains several of the main documents and these will be of great use to the readers of the book.

Author

Preface

The UNESCO World Conference on Education for Sustainable Development—*Moving into the Second Half of the UN Decade of Education for Sustainable Development (2005-2014)* was held from 31 March to 2 April 2009 in Bonn, Germany. The Organisers of the Conference were the UNESCO and the German Federal Ministry of Education and Research in cooperation with the German Commission for UNESCO.

The Conference objectives were (1) to highlight the relevance of ESD to all of education; (2) to promote international exchange on ESD, especially between the north and the south; (3) to carry out a stocktaking of the implementation of the UN Decade; and (4) to develop strategies for the way ahead.

The participants of the Conference exchanged the best practices on Education for Sustainable Development from all the regions of the world. They developed mechanisms for enhanced cooperation in the implementation of the UN Decade of Education for Sustainable Development (2005-2014), especially focussing on the exchange between developing countries, those in transition and industrialised countries. Furthermore the participants discussed regional, national and cultural differences as well as challenges in the implementation of the UN Decade. At the end of the Conference, a Declaration reflecting the debates and proposing guidelines for the implementation of the UN Decade in its second half was adopted.

The book contains several of the main documents and these will be of great use to the readers of the book.

Author

Acknowledgements

I am thankful to the *UNESCO* and to the *German Federal Ministry of Education and Research* for reproducing the copy-right-free documents related to the *UNESCO World Conference on Education for Sustainable Development* held from 31 March to 2 April 2009 in Bonn, Germany, and also to the Deutsche UNESCO-Kommission e.V. German Commission for UNESCO Commission Allemande pour I'UNESCO for its cooperation to the success of the Conference.

I am very much grateful to Mr. Koïchiro Matsuura, from Director-General of UNESCO for reproducing his Welcome Address delivered at the 'UNESCO World Conference on Education for Sustainable Development' in order to give the readers the international view about the Conference.

I am also thankful to all the authors, authorities and dignitaries who were responsible for preparing the documents of 'UNESCO World Conference on Education for Sustainable Development'.

Dr. Digumarti Bhaskara Rao
digmartibhaskararao@rediffmail.com
Tele-Mobile +919493333555

Contents

PART—III
PROJECT-BASED WORKSHOPS

PART—I

UNESCO WORLD CONFERENCE ON EDUCATION FOR SUSTAINABLE DEVELOPMENT

CHAPTER

UNESCO World Conference on Education for Sustainable Development

The "World Conference on Education for Sustainable Development—Moving into the Second Half of the UN Decade" marks the midpoint of the United Nations Decade for Education for Sustainable Development. It is organized by UNESCO and the German Federal Ministry of Education and Research, in cooperation with the German Commission for UNESCO.

The conference will provide a platform for dialogue and advocacy on ESD at the global level. Some 700 participants from all regions will attend, representing UNESCO Member States, UN agencies, civil society organizations, youth and the private sector.

The World Conference on ESD comes at a time when education is increasingly recognized as a motor for change. And change—a massive reorientation of the ways people all over the world think and act—is required to ensure a sustainable future. The conference will be a major opportunity to highlight the role ESD must play in this process.

The Conference has four main goals:

— *To underline ESD's essential contribution to all education and to achieving quality education*

"Why is ESD relevant?"

— *To promote international exchange on ESD*

"What can we learn from each other? "

— To assess *DESD implementation*

"What have we achieved so far, what are the lessons learnt? "

Empirical results as well as global and regional reports from the first Monitoring and Evaluation exercise—currently being conducted by UNESCO—will provide input.

— *To develop strategies for the future*

"Where do we want to go from here?"

Major recommendations resulting from the Conference will be expressed in a Bonn Declaration. More detailed results (from plenary sessions, workshops and other conference events) will be made available in a post-conference publication.

WHAT IS EDUCATION FOR SUSTAINABLE DEVELOPMENT?

In Tuvalu, islanders involved in the Small is Beautiful project are being trained to tackle environmental problems threatening their survival. The San development programme in southern Africa brings not just schooling but also food, clothing and health facilities to a marginalized population. The international YouthXchange project distributes a teachers' toolkit designed to make sustainable lifestyles attractive to young people. These initiatives are all facets of the UN Decade of Education for Sustainable Development (DESD, 2005-2014).

Education for Sustainable Development (ESD) seeks to integrate the values and practices of sustainable development into all aspects of education.

The definition of sustainable development given by the World Commission on Environment and Development ("Brundtland Commission", 1987) remains valid: "Sustainable development is development that meets the needs of the present without compromising the ability of future generations to meet their own needs."

With persisting global patterns of poverty and inequality, along with emerging issues such as the impact of climate change and the current financial and economic crises, Sustainable development is a central challenge facing the world today.

Achieving sustainable development requires a global change of mindset and behaviours, for which education is a key prerequisite.

ESD is thus a comprehensive package for quality education and learning within which key issues—social tolerance, gender equality, poverty reduction, environmental protection, natural resource conservation, corporate social responsibility, prevention of HIV/AIDS, protection of indigenous cultures, etc.—are addressed.

ESD is a life-long undertaking starting from childhood, through formal schooling and throughout adulthood. ESD is relevant not only to formal education settings, training and workplace learning but also to public awareness—raising and many kinds of non-formal and informal learning.

In whatever setting, ESD encourages an interdisciplinary and holistic approach to teaching and learning and promotes critical and creative thinking in the educational process. It therefore implies new ways of teaching and learning.

UNITED NATIONS DECADE OF EDUCATION FOR SUSTAINABLE DEVELOPMENT

In December 2002, by Resolution 59/237, the UN General Assembly declared the years 2005-2014 the UN Decade of Education for Sustainable Development (DESD). Member States thus made a commitment to integrate the principles, values and practices of sustainable development into education and learning. The UN General Assembly designated UNESCO the lead agency for the global implementation and coordination of the DESD.

As the International Implementation Scheme for the DESD (US, 2005), states: "The basic vision of the DESD is a world where everyone has the opportunity to benefit from education and learn the values, behaviour and lifestyles required for a Sustainable future and for positive societal transformation."

The IIS proposes four main objectives for the DESD: to facilitate networking and exchange among stakeholders in ESD; to foster increased quality of teaching and learning in ESD; to help countries attain the Millennium Development Goals through ESD efforts; and to provide countries with new opportunities to incorporate ESD into education reform efforts.

To approach the development of ESD initiatives holistically, four main directions have been identified: facilitating access to quality education; re-orienting existing education systems to address sustainability concerns; launching public awareness and understanding initiatives; and establishing training programmes to address specific social, environmental and economic sustainability issues.

The DESD must be viewed in relation to other international priorities in development and education. The Millennium Development Goals (MDGs) provide the relevant framework for international development cooperation; the six Education for All (EFA) goals aim at extending the reach of basic education to everyone; and the United Nations Literacy Decade (UNLD) focuses on the contribution of youth and adult literacy to building knowledge societies in which all may participate. Oriented towards the goal of sustainable development, the DESD focuses specifically on the content and purpose of education and learning.

UNESCO'S ROLE IN ESD DECADE

UNESCO's role as lead agency for the DESD is in line with its past involvement in sustainable development, its mandates and its function as laboratory of ideas, standard-setter, clearing house, capacity-builder and international cooperation promoter. All parts of UNESCO work together in an intersectoral manner.

As global coordinator of the DESD, UNESCO is working to:

- catalyze new partnerships with the private sector, youth and media groups;
- encourage a research agenda on ESD;
- serve as forum for bringing together key stakeholders, such as multinationals, faith-based institutions, indigenous people, etc.;
- share good ESD practices;
- link Member States that have put in place ESD curricula, policies and research with those Member States requesting help
- establish global frameworks and mechanisms to ensure effective monitoring and assessment of DESD implementation
- convene working groups on specific ESD topics;
- provide strategic guidance.

UNESCO's actions around the world

UNESCO has established coordination mechanisms, such as the Inter-Agency Committee for the DESD and a Monitoring and Evaluation Expert Group. UNESCO Regional Offices are playing a key role—UNESCO Bangkok, for example, has set up an Asia Pacific regional inter-agency committee and organized consultations. UNESCO National Commissions have helped launch national Decade committees.

At national level, Cluster and Field offices have helped Member States implement ESD. For instance, UNESCO Brazilia has provided technical assistance to the Brazilian government within the Education Development Plan (PDE), to develop programmes that include ESD in basic education, higher education, vocational education and literacy.

UNESCO has in addition prepared a variety of web-based tools, information and print materials. Vision-building has also taken the form of school contests, awards, ESD-related projects (essays, debates, income-generating projects) as well as joint school and community DESD initiatives.

UNESCO's Associated Schools (8000 schools in 177 countries) are initiating regional and international intercultural projects within the DESD framework (such as the Baltic Sea Project, the Great Volga River Route Project, or the Western Mediterranean Sea Project). Their activities encourage deeper understanding of issues associated with sustainable development—poverty, environmental degradation, population growth, urban and rural transformation, health, cultural diversity etc.

Partnerships have been established and synergies created between programmes and initiatives. UNESCO has entered into a number of partnerships or joint actions with sister UN agencies (in particular with UNEP and UN-Habitat), civil society partners, the private sector, media professionals, and faith-based organizations.

So far so good: highlights from the First DESD Global Progress Report

Since the start of the DESD, many activities have been undertaken by a broad range of stakeholders. National Committees have been set up, networks have been established, education materials have been developed and disseminated, good practices have been highlighted and shared, and meetings have been organized to encourage international exchange.

By the end of 2008, at least 73 countries in the world had a national ESD coordinating body, up from 44 at the end of 2006.

Worldwide, there is a notable presence of ESD in national policy documents.

Much remains to be done, however, before ESD occupies a truly central place in educational and learning processes and fulfils its potential to improve education quality.

INTERVIEW WITH CHARLES HOPKINS, UNESCO CHAIR IN EDUCATION FOR SUSTAINABLE DEVELOPMENT, YORK UNIVERSITY, CANADA BY FARID GARDIZI, DEPUTY SPOKESPERSON, GERMAN COMMISSION FOR UNESCO

***Farid Gardizi*: The financial market crisis is a typical example of missing Sustainable Development. Are you optimistic about the future of the world?**

Charles Hopkins: For so many of the world's poor it's a disaster. So I am not very optimistic. But the good news is we realize that we can't just suddenly switch from focussing on the environment to addressing the economy or social issues, each in isolation, as in the past. This time we are capable of looking at the market in a concerted way through the concept of sustainable development. So I am optimistic that we could make a better recovery. In the meantime it's going to be very, very hard on many on the world's poor.

***Gardizi:* Who lags behind so far? Is it more society, the economy or politics?**

Hopkins: From an ESD perspective I would say it is society in general. Many countries around the world don't have an integrated ESD or even an effective SD strategy. The society in these countries is often not engaged. In other countries we are finding that the general society has not been exposed to sustainability at all. But we need the ESD public awareness and understanding programmes. We need training programmes at all levels and we need better education programmes that deal with the real sustainability issues. Once we have an informed society we can better address the environmental and economic issues in a more equitable and informed manner.

***Gardizi:* Schools are an important interface for education for sustainable development. If young people acquire the knowledge and values, they have the chance to think and act with lasting effect. So how can students best learn to understand the exceedingly abstract subject of sustainability?**

Hopkins: One of the best ways is by not calling it sustainability, especially with younger students. ESD has to deal with the students' and teachers' real issues such as sharing, caring and relating, before you slowly move from a 'me' focus to a 'we' focus. Dealing with their own local environmental and social issues first and then slowly building up to a global perspective is a workable entry for schools. An important component of formal education's engagement with ESD is using ESD to address the existing academic goals. *Access* and *Retention* in quality education is a shared thrust of ESD and school systems. Using sustainability issues to enhance critical thinking skills is but one of many examples of overlapping objectives. To begin, we should focus on age appropriate competences. These competences go beyond factual knowledge and include skills, values, perceptions and action skills. ESD however is 'place-based' and must also be developed in a locally relevant and culturally appropriate manner.

***Gardizi:* What are good ESD practices at school level?**

Hopkins: One place to start is the curriculum. What is being taught and modelled? If we are trying to promote democracy, we must model democracy in the classroom. What kind of governance models do we have in the school itself? These are the sort of surface things that would be good practices. But also there are much deeper ones: What do we fund or timetable? What do we evaluate and what do we report upon? What is it that our whole school system models in its purchasing, school meals and buildings? The system must declare ESD a priority, fund it, measure its progress and report upon achievements. That way the teachers, students and school officials will know that ESD truly is important and not just another peripheral add-on.

***Gardizi:* Do you think that the teachers have already realized how important education for sustainable development is?**

Hopkins: Usually they intuitively understand and agree. But they often say there is no time in the curriculum, there are no resources. Some teachers think it's just another societal issue for schools to deal with without training or fiscal or human resources. To change this, we really need to engage the senior education leaders. They have to understand ESD, be mandated and resourced to develop strategic, concerted implementation plans. We also need to work with parents and the entire community as they don't know yet what ESD is trying to accomplish. So we have to work both from the top down and the bottom up.

***Gardizi:* What could be extra steps to ensure that the important role of education for sustainable development is emphasized more strongly?**

Hopkins: One major step needed is to ensure that at least the new teachers will have competences in ESD. There are 60 million teachers now in the world. We just don't have funding to retrain them all. But we certainly can be working with the faculties producing the new teachers. We need to engage those institutions and the ministries that direct them. UNESCO knows this and is working hard with countries and institutions to address this issue.

***Gardizi:* What do you expect from the World Conference in Bonn?**

Hopkins: The first thing is a more informed senior leadership in our ministries worldwide. If they are to redirect policy and resources, they have to understand what ESD is, both currently and its potential. This would be a tremendous asset on its own. Secondly, I expect that we will be surprised to see all that is going on around the world in ESD right now and to celebrate our gains. Thirdly, I expect we will have some agreement on concerted work plans in various sectors and regions that engage people at all levels. Lastly, I expect that we will come out of the Conference reinvigorated, with BSD as a priority worth funding, and with the willingness to work synergistically for the remaining years of the Decade and beyond.

PROJECTS

Chanuka Express

By Yvonne Otieno and *Susan Scrull-Carvalho*

An older man was walking along the beach and came upon a sandy stretch where thousands of starfish had washed ashore.

Just ahead, he spotted a teenager picking up starfish one at a time and tossing them back into the ocean.

"Oh! You're being silly!" he exclaimed. "You can't possibly save *all* of these starfish. There are too many!"

Smiling the teenager replied, "I know. But I can save this one," and she tossed another into the ocean, "and this one'", toss, "and this one, and..."

Each and every one of our acts of caring and taking responsibility is critical.

This is the message Chanuka Express is spreading among young people—both in and out of school: always do the 'right thing' because we can make a difference! And young people *CAN* ... and ***ARE*** doing just that. They're realizing that this is

our life and ***our*** world and they're learning—one step at a time—how to take care of it for their life and for future generations too.

In Kiswahili Chanuka means to *"Get with it or 'bloom ' by using knowledge."* This is a youth-centred learning and capacity-building motivational programme based on the *Young African Express* educational newspaper and the principles *of Education for Sustainable Development* or ESD. As a partnership between UNESCO and the newspaper's publisher, Jacaranda Designs—with help from the private sector including Tetra Pak and Shell—it's a mobile outreach training programme operating out of a bus —the *Chanuka* Express. Our slogan is *Maisha Yetu, Dunia Yetu* (Our Life, Our World) and the theme is *'Learning for Sustainable Living.'*

Reaching teenagers in low-income primary schools and communities, the programme focuses on smaller groups of peer-selected Chanuka Club leaders and trains and prepares them to create and share messages and skills with others. These young leaders *identify their own* priority issues of personal safety, health, hygiene, water and sanitation, and environmental degradation. Confronted by the harsh realities of poverty, violence and joblessness, the *Chanuka* facilitators are helping young people realize how much they already know and how capable they are in sharpening their skills and using these to inspire themselves, their peers and other people in taking responsibility for improving their *quality of life*—despite tough multiple challenges.

Like the young woman with the starfish, their level of determination is making an impact not only on them but on their communities, schools and families too. Sustainable development in our country is depending on them: on young people equipped with productive knowledge, practical skills and a positive character.

Through open honest discussions, participatory training and interactive learning support, young people are choosing to be 'agents of change.' By learning and using their knowledge, practical life skills and capabilities of motivating and inspiring action for positive change, they are choosing *Chanuka!*—or *to Get with it!*

A day in the life of Chanuka

In the morning, Chanuka facilitators—a trained and motivated team of young adult volunteers, mostly university students—climb aboard the Chanuka Express bound for the day's venue. With them is a raft of teaching tools, props, and art supplies. Among these tools are copies of the *Young African Express,* a monthly educational newspaper aligned to the Kenyan curriculum and filled with illustrated articles, cartoons, facts and games focussing on essential life skills.

On arrival, they meet up with a pre-selected group of teenagers from schools and youth clubs in the area. Teachers and other members of the community are there too. After a short highly participatory puppet show or community theatre introduction, the youth form four Chanuka teams—Peace and Safety, Health, Water and Sanitation, and the Environment.

In small groups, the young people engage in games, demonstrations, discovery sessions, role-plays and discussions to identify key local challenges and solutions. These young leaders form the backbone of the Chanuka Clubs set up in every school involved. The day ends with presentations of the identified key issues and the action plans made by each group.

The Chanuka Express visits each site 2-3 times a year. Between visits, the young people and teachers are not idle. They form Chanuka Clubs with Health, Water and Sanitation, Safety and Peace, and Environment teams. The teams recruit others in their schools, passing on the messages they created and mobilizing others to join in taking action on important issues. They record their plans, obstacles and successes in supplied notebooks and these are used by the Chanuka facilitators on return visits to assess their progress and assist with problem-solving.

The results are impressive. Chanuka Club members at Evangel Primary School in Baba Dogo, Nairobi realised there was a high rate of absenteeism at their school, which was affecting the pupils' performance.

The club members investigated and found out that pupils were missing school due to stomach ache. They connected the stomach aches to worms caused by unhygienic habits including eating with unwashed hands and drinking unsafe water.

The club's solution was to help pupils and teachers understand this health issue and how to help themselves. They started a de-worming campaign in the school.

First they raised awareness using information and they held discussions with their schoolmates to motivate action. To feel better, they needed to get rid of the worms by taking de-worming tablets. To buy these, they came up with a plan—they asked every member of their school community to donate Ksh 20 to the project.

Their parents were so impressed by the idea that they contributed more money, and the club was soon able to buy de-worming tablets for the entire school community—children, teenagers and the adult teachers!

Water schools shed light on Yangtze pollution

By Gong Yidong

Water is a daily necessity for most people, but it is a constant companion to primary school student Sun Yao in southwest China's Sichuan Province.

He has lived alongside Baicao River, a tributary of the Yangtze, the largest river in China and the third longest in the world, for more than 12 years.

At the upper reaches of Yangtze, the Baicao River provides drinking water to the 6,600 inhabitants of Piankou Town, Beichuan County, which was among the most severely damaged during the May 12 Wenchuan earthquake that claimed more than 80,000 lives. However, the *Mother River* has seen a drastic change over the last two decades.

In the 1980s, it was "so clear that you could see to the bottom", recalls Zeng Wenjun, a town resident in his forties.

"The Qingbo *(Clean Water)* Fish exclusive to the river was unmatchable in taste, but it is now regrettably extinct."

Sun was concerned about the foul-smelling 'rubbish mountains' along the 10-km river, piles of polyfoams, cupboard cups, food scraps, medical needles and tubes, and plastic bags.

The run-off from private gold mines and sandstone collectors adds to the filth. The mushrooming small and medium-sized hydropower stations also pose an ecological risk to the livelihoods of the people living nearby.

The 1,000-plus towns along the upper reaches of the Yangtze pump the numerous tributaries with waste, causing a huge environmental problem at the Three Gorges Dam, says Fu Zhiping, a professor of ecology at Mianyang Normal University, Sichuan.

The Yangtze river system produces 40 per cent of the nation's grain, a third of its cotton, 48 per cent of its freshwater fish and 40 per cent of the total industrial output value. However, it is also a depository for 60 per cent of the country's pollution, making it the single largest source of pollution in the Pacific Ocean, according to Shangri-la Institute for Sustainable Communities (SISC), a Chinese non-governmental organization.

In the spring of 2008, both Sun and Fu took part in the *Water School for a Living Yangtze* under the *International Water School Programme* sponsored by Austria's Swarovski company, a programme that also includes the Nile in Egypt and India's Ganges.

The Chinese programme, supervised by the SISC, with the Ministry of Education and UNESCO as its partners, has involved more than 50,000 students from 27 middle and primary schools in Sichuan and the adjacent provinces of Qinghai and Yunnan, as well as Shanghai, where the Yangtze meets the East China Sea.

Under the guidance of teacher Tang Ming, Sun and his classmates at Piankou Central Primary School began to monitor water quality by using graduated cylinders and test papers, which they had never used before. The preliminary test result confirmed Sun's concerns: the PH index stands at 5.8 at the lower reaches of Baicao River, with the turbidity reaching Grade IV, showing that the water has already been polluted to an alarming extent.

Based on further investigations in and around Piankou Town, Sun and his classmates proposed in a written letter to re-arrange the 15 dustbins along the two major streets 'in a more scientific way' and establish a rubbish disposal system.

To their great surprise, the town government approved their proposal, and a sewage treatment plant based on the scientific principles of a biological wetland is also under discussion.

The students also disseminated questionnaires to the communities of Piankou, and 89 per cent of the respondents believed it was necessary to treat the river pollution.

"The project provides a platform for effective environmental protection around the branches of Yangtze, and it is a model for shifting away from the exam-focussed educational system," says Fu, who has 14 years' experience in the field of environmental education.

The water schools on the Yangtze have gone beyond the boundaries of campuses to complement local social, economic and cultural conditions.

For instance, the lamas of Dongzhulin Temple, in Deqing Tibetan Autonomous Prefecture in Yunnan, are invited to contribute to water protection through their religious teachings that link nature and man.

"The value of this project lies in its integrated model that involves the communities over a broad spectrum, instead of a technical solution targeting a minor issue. We encourage the process of learning by doing, so that a tangible change in mindsets and behaviour will impact the policy-making of government, which promotes wider public participation in long-term environmental protection," says Dorjie, SISC programme coordinator.

In 2009, the project will expand to China's capital Beijing, a city notorious for its scarcity of water. Besides the *Education for Sustainable Development on the Tibet Plateau* project surrounding the Yalu Tsangpo River, the SISC is also aiming to carry out a similar environmental education project along China's second longest river, the Yellow River, says Dorjie.

Everyone knows Facebook—but do you know Solar Net International?

By Bianca Bilgram

"Solarnet is not only a website, but a community where people, countries, thinkings are connected. It is like a whole-packaged visual travelling, offering new friendships, knowledge and experience; yet costs you nothing."

Through the internet, the world is just one click away. To make 'the world' more tangible an international exchange forum was established by a group of students and teachers at the Schiller gymnasium in Münster, Germany, in 2005. The internet platform was named Solar Net International and has set itself the aim to improve the inter-cultural competence of young learners and at the same time to encourage their media and communication skills and environmental awareness. Since 2005 over 1400 students and young learners from more than

90 countries have registered to be part of the Solar Net Network. Solar Net International has since grown from a school project to a globally active non-governmental organisation, registered as an association in Germany and Poland. The network provides people with a platform for inter-cultural exchange by initiating and supporting various educational, environmental and social projects in its partner countries. Members communicate and cooperate with each other daily through the communication board.

What makes Solar Net special?

The main pedagogic interest of the project is to motivate young people from different cultures and backgrounds to share their lives and ideas with each other. The appeal is that it is quite simple for members to post reports for one another, especially relaying their everyday lives. With a wide range of topics covered in these reports, and the potential for feedback and discussion, the report system at Solar Net compliments the aims of global learning. Through the reporting, new perspectives and insights into other cultures can be gained, and it reflects how perceptions of other countries and cultures are often influenced by media or stereotypes that do not represent the daily life of other cultures. One unique component of this project is the fact that each participant—regardless of age, gender, colour, or culture—is both a student and a teacher.

The reports and discussion topics also initiate enthusiasm and participants gain motivation to present themselves, their culture, their language, their environment or any topic that is of importance to them. In this way, the project engenders a natural curiosity for topics of personal significance and at the same time generates awareness for important issues that have been brought up by other members. Global, political, environmental, and religious topics are discussed and common and differing point of views shared.

Learning each others' language at the same time...

Learning a foreign language is the first step to understand and to exchange with other cultures. In our modern world cross-cultural competence and foreign language skills gain more and more importance. Since 2007 Solar Net produces regularly video language courses, so far with the focus on German and Polish language, although courses have been published in 14 other languages which can be seen on Solar Net TV. All those video language courses are published on Youtube: www.youtube.com/magauchsein. Through this tool new users are introduced to the network and the network grows continuously.

Solar Net encourages its members from all around the world to produce video language courses for their partners and in its languages forum its members plan new video language courses, help each other with learning languages and form online learning groups.

Initiating educational, environmental and social projects in partner countries

At local level members of Solar Net work together on media, environmental and language projects and share expertise and experience when developing new projects and implementing them. For example: through local media workshops in schools members help young learners to gain multimedia skills and learn how to photograph, film, record audio sounds and how to use graphic-and video-editing programmes, which are then posted on the website.

One example: School village Baumgartsbrunn in Namibia

The school village of Baumgartsbrunn in the Khomas Highland of Namibia consists of the Primary School Baumgartsbrunn (state primary school) and the Institute for Domestic Science and Agriculture (domestic vocational school for young women).

The school village, founded 30 years ago by the German couple Helmut and Gertraude Bleks, is now, among others, supported by several groups from Solar Net. The association of Solar Net International has been involved for several years namely in the fields of renewable energies and international youth exchange. The association supported the installation of a photovoltaic station in the vocational school and the installation of a solarthermic warm water supply in the primary school, which, since last year, has been providing more than 300 pupils with warm water for the first time.

The basic idea of the project is to bring together young students from Namibia and Germany through the internet platform and school exchange trips. In the past years, five successful youth exchanges with students from Baumgartsbrunn and Münster could be realized. Not only do these meetings of students help to fight prejudices and develop mutual understanding for the relevant cultures, but they also promote motivation and social commitment in all participants.

Common projects like films, presentations and exhibitions helped Solar Net to provide information and to acquire sponsorship, donations of material and money for the improvement of living conditions of the people in Baumgartsbrunn. By extending the internet access of Baumgartsbrunn and establishing a Namibia Forum in February 2006, a public communication platform could be initiated on Solar Net international.

Encouraging youngsters...

Since 2007 Solar Net also provides a Junior Area on its website, enabling the internet-based exchange of young students (up to age of 16) worldwide.

The project is supported by teachers in Germany, Namibia and Poland. The students are given a task every month, which they have to complete together through the help of the internet and the Solar Net network. Besides intercultural exchange and environmental awareness raising the aim is also to encourage their media and communication skills in general but also to continue expanding the scope of Solar Net International.

The Swiss International Teachers' Programme

By Dr Lawrence Byrnes

What do 300 wonderful teachers from Brazil, Canada, South Africa, Vietnam, USA, and Switzerland have in common? They all participated in the SITP, an unforgettable educational and social experience at an American university where they studied and played together while learning about the inter-relationship of the economy, ecology, and society. They met with teachers, politicians, business owners and citizens to learn about the local community and issues they face. They took fascinating field trips to get an up close and personal feel for the sights and sounds of the environment and the culture of the area.

Participants selected an action team to role play and solve problems of a fictitious country called ECOLAND ravaged by pollution and poor decisions by government, households, and business. They used a computer simulation programme called ECOSYS, which is a macroeconomics software programme that allows participants to realize the cumulative impact of their decisions on the quality of life of the citizens of ECOLAND. One goal of the SITP originators was to have participants return home and change the way they teach their students.

Participants invested several weeks of their summer holidays to engage in lively debates about how to build a sustainable future locally, nationally, and globally. They learned the necessity of listening to others and practiced letting go of biases to reach consensus. Indeed, some participants from the summer 2000 programme are still communicating and visiting each other. Others have taken what they learned back home and implemented projects and programmes based on the knowledge and skills acquired at the SITP.

One Swiss participant from the 2005 programme expressed her feelings as follows:

> "After attending the SITP, I regularly e-mail Brazil, South Africa, and Florida. But there are other things too. First, I'm going to give some presentations on the occasion of our team meeting. I'm going to talk about ECOSYS, the hot topics such as bullying and diversity at schools. Second, I changed the first topic in the subject: people and their environment. Normally, I started the new school year with the learner's improvement of language skills. But after SITP 05 I started with: 'I am responsible for my own learning and response-able to the success of the group.... Finally, the Brazilians are tremendously interested in the peacemaker project at our semi-independent state school. To sum up, my time in Florida was great and I learned a lot. Thanks."

Evaluation and improvement were keys to success. Each week participants completed a survey so we could make rapid improvements to our services. In addition, the results of a course-end formal evaluation were analyzed to make programmatic changes for the following year. One participant's comment has been a common theme for eight summers:

"Referring to your question about the impact of your excellent programme, I can assure you that it has changed my whole outlook on life and teaching.

I am aware of my personal attitude towards political and environmental views....The key word sustainability must not only be used as an essential business-oriented word but also experienced, lived and believed in. This is exactly what I learned during those four wonderful weeks."

To fully appreciate the evolving success of the SITP over eight years, one must understand the complexities of the programme and the challenges of designing, implementing, and managing an international enterprise. The participants come from different nations, speak many languages, and possess different world views and cultural traditions. They leave home to live and study together for three or four weeks. During the programme they laugh and cry together, shop together, share transportation and living space, grapple with a difficult economics-based simulation game, and create democratic communities of learners within their living quarters. One participant captured the essence of the programme as follows:

> "I originally chose to come...because I saw it as a great opportunity to brush up on my English. I personally consider it as most important to do so...But then I realized that it was more important to have conversations with the Brazilians and the South Africans, because studying grammar is something that can be done in Switzerland as well, but there would be no one telling us about his time in the underground when the Apartheid still took place in South Africa, no one speaking about daily struggles being a divorced mum and so on....I definitely improved my speaking skills, and in addition to that got to learn a lot about other people's circumstances of life."

The programme was launched at Florida Gulf Coast University and had a very successful six years tenure before being transferred to Virginia Tech University. A significant factor in the programme's success at both institutions has been strong partnerships with the School of Education at the Zurich University of Applied Sciences, and the Swiss business partner Holcim Inc. These close working relationships created energy and the teamwork necessary to anticipate and respond to changing circumstances. The SITP legacy will live on in 2009 as teachers throughout the world converge on Virginia Tech University for life changing experiences.

Project-based Workshops at the World Conference on Education for Sustainable Development

In the afternoon of the second day of the conference, all participants will be invited to participate in a workshop at an ESD project in the region. The aim of the project-based workshops is to strengthen the international exchange of good practice. Project-based workshops are organised by local ESD projects and will focus on the implementation of ESD in practice. Examples from Germany will be showcased through discussions and with hands-on experiences. In addition, project presentations and guided tours around the project area will be provided. Project-based workshops will also provide space for informal exchange between project representatives and conference participants.

I—Relevance of ESD for key sustainable development challenges

Water as a source of life: From traditional excursions to streams towards innovative stewardship of streams by schools.

Bonn

This project-based workshop will focus on projects with the aim of increasing knowledge on water as a source of life. Participants will be divided into smaller groups and rotate between three stations. The Erich Klausener Gymnasium will present its active role within a stewardship of streams which has been in operation for more than ten years: aquatic, solid and cultural-historical problems are thematised within the classroom and through field work. As a second station, the Nature and Biodiversity Conservation Union will offer active experiences with water through the participation in experiments and practices as well as the introduction of methods related to real-life activities. The NEPTUN (new partnership for transnational understanding and co-operation in water management) project will showcase as a third station its contribution to the further development of professionals in the water management field, via development of concepts, curricula and learning content based on the European Water Framework Directive.

Water quality and research—the ship MS Burgund as a swimming classroom

MS Burgund on the river Rhine

This project-based workshop will be conducted by the Ministry for Environment, Forest and Consumer Protection of the federal state of Rhine land-Palatinate. It takes place on the research ship 'MS Burgund' on the river Rhine. Workshop participants will take part in hands-on experiences normally conducted with school classes. Stations of learning with their exercises and working material specially created as a concept of teaching and learning within secondary schools will be presented to the workshop participants. These stations are guided by authentic experts like the ship's captain and the operator of the ship who normally present the stations to students. The project-based workshop wants to educate participants towards being 'laboratory assistants' 'stream researchers', 'discoverers of the Rhine' and 'ship's masters'.

Biological Diversity and Education for Sustainable Development.

Bonn University Botanic Gardens, Bonn

This project-based workshop is offered by the German Federal Agency for Nature Conservation (BfN), the Bonn University Botanic Gardens and Inwent Capacity Building International. The aim is to come into contact with colleagues of different countries and different backgrounds and talk about Biological Diversity as a key theme for ESD. Biological diversity in this context encompasses the conservation of species and habitats as well as a sustainable use. The great potential of Botanic Gardens and similar institutions for ESD in this context will be shown. On stations in the Botanic Gardens, small groups will discuss with project representatives about experiences in their own countries and opportunities for cooperation.

Learning sustainability in Forests and Nature—Examples of good practice in Germany.

German Hunting and Conservation Association, Bonn

Forests are an ideal place to demonstrate the principles of sustainability: Here, nature inspires one with regard to a great variation of topics. The core of forest and nature education is to foster an understanding with all senses, based on Pestalozzi's idea of learning with 'head, heart and hands'. Forest education combines more than one educational method and has the potential to teach essential competences for a sustainable development. Moreover, the principle of sustainability will be shown through examples of forest use, e.g. forestry and hunting. In innovative projects, sustainability is a process of negotiating ecological, economic, social and cultural factors. In the project-based workshop, four projects of interdisciplinary teaching outside of schools in and about forests will be presented.

II. Building partnerships to promote ESD

From research to action: implementing ESD in higher education.

German Academic Exchange Service, Bonn

Due to the summer school hosted by the German Academic Exchange Service (DAAD), 50 experts from different developing countries will get together in order to address the question as to how universities can actively face up to the challenges associated with ESD, and to what extent targeted structural changes can contribute to transforming universities for sustainability. In order to address varied experiences, as well as to emphasize cultural and regional issues, two topics will be presented, namely: "Sustainable Development as Strategy and Aim of Higher Education" (University of Lüneburg) and "From Research to Practice: The Role of Education for Sustainable Development in Natural Resource Management in Research, Education and International

Cooperation" (University of Greifswald). Cross-border education and cross-cultural experiences will be interactively discussed with the audience and the conference delegates. In cooperation with the United Nations University (UNU) this workshop fosters a diverse platform in order to empower international experts on this agenda. With this instrument, the DAAD summer school on ESD, aims to encourage an interdisciplinary and holistic approach in the field of ESD.

ESD and the socio-economic dimensions: a challenge towards changing behaviours and consumption patterns.
German Academic Exchange Service, Bonn

Due to the summer school hosted by the German Academic Exchange Service (DAAD), 50 experts from different developing countries will get together in order to address the question as to how universities can actively face up to the challenges associated with ESD, and to what extent targeted structural changes can contribute to transforming universities for sustainability. In order to address varied experiences, as well as to emphasize cultural and regional issues, two topics will be presented, namely: "Poverty and Social Inequality in Education and its Impact on Sustainable Development" (University of Kassel) and "Sustainability within the organic chemistry lab course" (University of Braunschweig). Cross-border education and cross-cultural experiences will be interactively discussed with the audience and the conference delegates. This workshop fosters a diverse platform in order to empower international experts on this agenda. With this instrument, the DAAD summer school on ESD, aims to encourage an interdisciplinary and holistic approach in the field of ESD.

How to approach global justice? Methods and instruments enhancing global competences and understanding.

Inwent - Capacity Building International, Bonn

This workshop invites the participants to get involved in a direct dialogue: In the framework of this workshop, participants will learn about different approaches to education for sustainable development covering different target and age groups, including persons with disabilities. All participants will have the opportunity to interact with different methods and instruments to achieve an interesting intercultural and transgenerational dialogue on global justice. An exhibition presenting the different methods and instruments accompanies this workshop.

III. Capacity Development for ESD

ESD and ICT: Multimedia learning.

Wissenschaftsladen, Bonn

Multimedia and learning with ICT is becoming more and more important day-by-day. In this project-based workshop, different models of learning through multimedia for ESD will be introduced. A brief introduction will present the different models of ICT-based learning. Participants will then have the possibility to have hands-on experience at the different projects within a large exhibition together with representatives of projects. After this, a discussion on the process of learning through multimedia in different countries will be held.

Non-formal Education for Sustainable Development through Experiential Learning.

Finkens Garden, Cologne

Finkens Garden is an eco-social natural garden of 50,000 m^2 where pre-school and primary school children can experience nature with hands-on experiences and senses. Within the project-based workshop, there will be a guided tour through the project area as well as the presentation of four partner projects from the city of Aalen, Aalen University, the BUND-Centre Heilbronn and the Society for Environmental Education Baden-Wiirttemberg. Participants will discuss the orientation of ESD towards experience and how to foster the interest of people of all ages for environmental topics by means of experimental learning, e.g. sowing, planting and harvesting as well as sensory experiences such as seeing, hearing, smelling, tasting and feeling; also in contact to natural elements like air, soil and water—by actively discovering and taking action.

Non-formal Education for Sustainable Development in visitor centres, exhibitions and nature experience activities.

Naturgut Ophoven, Leverkusen

This project-based workshop focuses on non-formal learning. Three stations will deal with ESD at exhibitions and nature experience activities. The International Wadden Sea School (IWSS) is an educational programme for school classes from the Wadden Sea countries Denmark, Germany and The Netherlands. It wants to put into effect the idea of a trans-boundary approach to the protection of the Wadden Sea with the younger generation. The Germanwatch Climate Expedition brings climate change, its impacts and solutions into the class rooms by the means of live satellite images. By viewing the Earth from space, one can compare the situation of polar ice, glaciers, lakes, rainforests and other ecosystems in former times to their actual conditions. The project-based workshop takes place in NaturGut Ophoven, one of the greatest points for extra-curricular environmental education in the federal state of North Rhine-Westphalia. It has a big innovative exhibition on the topic of energy and a natural site with demonstration habitats of over 60,000 square metres. It works with schools, kindergartens and adults.

IV—ESD and the teaching-learning process

UNESCO Associated Schools working towards ESD.

Robert Wetzlar Vocational School, Bonn

The German UNESCO ASPnet has 192 member schools of all types and age groups. The main topics of its work are Human Rights, Peace and Democracy Education, Intercultural Learning, Education for Sustainable Development and World Heritage Education, to name just a few. The Associated Schools use methods like open school, interdisciplinary classes, projects for different age groups and others to implement

UNESCO's aims and principles in their school programmes. Three ASP Schools will take part in the project-based workshop in Bonn. The Schiller gymnasium Münster will present Solar Net International, an association to support intercultural exchange projects. The Comenius Kolleg Mettingen will present group activities for first year university students based on ecological projects that were the results of German-Brazilian cooperation. The Robert Wetzlar Berufskolleg is the host school and will present projects on sustainable breakfast and barrier-free tourism within the region.

Pre-conference for the Children and Youth International Conference for the Environment (Brazil 2010).

Emilie Heyermann Secondary School, Bonn

The Project "50/50—energy efficiency and renewable energy" of the Emilie Heyermann Secondary School in Bonn is part of Agenda 21 at school and an official German project for the UN Decade. Students from Bonn and their partner schools in Budapest (Hungary) and Buchara (Uzbekistan) will set in motion working groups on the themes of climate change, energy efficiency, renewable energy, waste avoidance and prevention of violence. Workshops will take place as a Conference at School in the lead-up to the Children and Youth International Conference for the Environment to be hosted by Brazil in 2010. This conference is a pedagogical campaign that brings together both the participation and the environmental-political dimensions for education on the theme of global responsibility. Workshop participants will get involved in direct dialogue with the students discussing their ideas of projects to be started at the school.

Education for Sustainable Development in Life and at Work.

House of NICA (sustainability within chemical vocational training), Hürth

The House of NICA is a common pilot project of the Federal Institute for Vocational Education and Training (BIBB), the Institute for Innovation and Sustainability (IRIS) and the educational institution 'Rhine-Erft Academy', financially supported by the Federal Ministry of Education and Research. Starting with programmes like 'responsible care', there is a trend in the chemical industry towards developing a corporate culture. This goal can only be achieved with the participation of the whole staff. The pilot project NICA tries to transform the more abstract business principle of sustainable development into practical work. The pilot project is divided into the following sub-projects: development and testing of modules to integrate sustainability into VET; development and testing of a model of indicators and key figures to assess sustainability; 'House of NICA'—apprentices plan and construction of a sustainable house; The sustainable educational institution. Within the project-based workshop, the project will be presented by vocational students.

Starting strong: Education for Sustainable Development in early childhood.

Kindergarten 'Hand in Hand', Oberhonnefeld

This project-based workshop will show that skills and competences of fundamental importance can be nurtured long before the first day at school. The approach of 'Learning to shape life' has been implemented into everyday work at several hundred kindergartens within Germany. One of these, the day nursery in Oberhonnefelde, will discuss their work on ESD in early childhood through an exchange of ideas and experiences with participants. The implementation of this approach through information, cooperation, education, support and creativity within the federal State of Rhineland-Palatinate will be shown as well.

EDUCATION FOR SUSTAINABLE DEVELOPMENT RESOURCES

UNESCO DESD Website'. www.unesco.org/education/desd

Publications:

- UNESCO and Sustainable Development brochure **(http://unesdoc.unesco.org/images/0013/001393/139369e.pdf)**

- Linkages between global education initiatives **(http://unesdoc.unesco.org/images/0014/001408/140848m.pdf)**
- Guidelines and Recommendations for Reorienting Teacher Education to Address Sustainability **(http://unesdoc.unesco.org/images/0014/001433/143370e.pdf)**
- Good practices in education for sustainable development: teacher education institutions **(http://unesdoc.unesco.org/images/0015/001524/152452eo.pdf)**
- Good practices in the UN Economic Commission for Europe (UNECE) region **(http://unesdoc.unesco.org/iniages/0015/001533/153319e.pdf)**
- Education for Sustainable Development Toolkit **(http://unesdoc.unesco.org/images/0015/001524/152453eo.pdf)**
- 'Teaching and Learning for a Sustainable Future' multimedia teacher education programme **(www.unesco.org/education/tlsf)**
- The DESD in brief leaflet **(http://unesdoc.unesco.org/images/0014/001416/141629e.pdf)**
- DESD International Implementation Scheme **(http://unesdoc.unesco.org/images/0014/001486/148654E.pdf)**
- Framework for the UN DESD International Implementation Scheme **(http://unesdoc.unesco.org/images/0014/001486/148650E.pdf)**
- International Implementation Scheme in brief (user friendly booklet) **(http://unesdoc.unesco.org/images/0014/001473/147361E.pdf)**

CHAPTER

How the Work of the Meeting Will Be Conducted?

This multistakeholder meeting is a Mid-decade review within UNESCO's role as the lead agency for the UN Decade on Education for Sustainable Development (DESD 2005-2014). Under the "Regulations for the general classification of the various categories of meetings convened by UNESCO", adopted by the General Conference at its 14th session (14/C resolution 23), this meeting is considered to be in Category IV: 'International Congress' and it is called:

"UNESCO World Conference on Education for Sustainable Development—Moving into the second half of the UN Decade".

The meeting shall take place from 31 March—2 April 2009 at the World Conference Center Bonn, Platz der Vereinten Nationen 2,53113 Bonn, Germany.

Organizers of the conference are UNESCO and the German Federal Ministry of Education and Research, in cooperation with the German Commission for UNESCO. The meeting has been organized by a Task Force composed of representatives from these three institutions.

As stipulated in article 45, § 2 of the Regulations mentioned above, "The Director-General may decide that rules of procedure are not necessary. In that case, an information paper giving the necessary details of the way in which the work of the meeting will be conducted shall be prepared and distributed."

Participants

Due to the limited space available at the Conference venue in Bonn, the number of participants will be limited to 700-800. They will be drawn from the following categories:

Category I: Specialists from UNESCO Member States serving in an individual capacity (275):

Ministers
Experts from the Ministry of Education
Experts from the National Commissions for UNESCO

Category II: Participants directly invited by the Conference Task Force (100):

Representatives from civil society, the private sector and UN Agencies as well as UNESCO stakeholders of the DESD: Monitoring and Evaluation Expert Group (MEEG), Inter-Agency Committee (IAC), Reference Group, International Advisory Group (IAG), etc.

Category III: Experts selected via an open call for applications (220):

Around 500 applications have been received and 300 selected applicants will have received an invitation by 20 February 2009.

Category IV: Organizing institutions (80):

Representatives from UNESCO, the German Government and institutions coordinating a workshop or having an active role in the Conference. **Youth (25):**

Participants in a workshop with 25 young people from around the world with demonstrated engagement in Education for Sustainable Development.

Objectives of the meeting

The World Conference on Education for Sustainable Development will pursue four main objectives:

1. To highlight the essential contribution of Education for Sustainable Development (ESD) to all of education and to achieving quality education
2. To promote international exchange on ESD
3. To carry out a stock-taking of DESD implementation
4. To develop strategies for the way ahead

Structure of the meeting

The meeting will comprise a High-Level Segment, plenary and workshop sessions, project-based workshops, special events and an exhibition of good practices. Each element will contribute to the four conference objectives.

The 22 workshops, which will take place parallel in two tranches of 11, are clustered along the four following themes:

1. Relevance of ESD for key Sustainable development challenge
2. Building partnerships for ESD
3. Capacity Development for ESD
4. ESD and the teaching-learning process

For more information, please consult the attached programme outline.

High-Level Segment

Only Ministers, Vice-Ministers and Heads of UN Agencies will be allowed to participate in the High-Level Segment. Vice-Ministers will only be allowed if no Minister from the country is present. Seating in the room will be in alphabetical order. Interpretation in the following languages will be provided: English, French, Spanish, Arabic, Chinese and German.

Assistants may enter the room before the official opening of the Segment but they may not stay after the beginning of the session. Assistants will be accommodated in another room in the same building during the time of the High-Level Segment. All other conference participants will take part in the regular workshops starting in the afternoon of 31 March.

The High-level Segment will be opened and co-chaired by the Director-General of UNESCO Mr. Koichiro Matsuura; the German Federal Minister of Education and Research, Ms. Annette Schavan; and the President of the Standing Conference of the Ministers of Education and Cultural Affairs of the Lander in the Federal Republic of Germany, Mr. Henry Tesch. Each will speak for no more than five minutes.

The formal opening of the session will be followed by five opening statements of approximately five minutes each made by six Ministers from different world regions invited by the Director-General. Subsequently, there will be a short break of ten minutes.

The second part of the segment will take the form of a moderated and interactive discussion among Ministers on the topic of Education for Sustainable Development and Quality Education. There will be no formal set-piece presentations by Ministers about their own countries' contributions. Ministers will act as respondents rather than as presenters. Mr. Nino Munoz Gomez (Director of the Bureau for Public Information, UNESCO) will be the moderator of the session and will call upon ministers to address key issues relevant to the theme of the session, notably: the main opportunities and key challenges associated with adopting and applying an ESD approach in educational policies, plans and programmes, especially in such areas as curriculum development and teacher education. In addition, discussion will consider the added value of an ESD approach towards achieving an improved quality of education. In order to give each Minister the chance to take part in the debate and to allow for a genuine discussion, it will be essential that participants respect the format and refrain from reading pre-written presentations.

Ministers who wish to do so may table a written government statement on ESD; such statements will be duplicated and made available to conference participants as well as placed on the conference website.

At the end of the session, the chairs will call upon one of the General Rapporteurs of the conference (Ms. Mary Joy Pigozzi, member of the Director-General's High-level Panel on the UN Decade of Education for Sustainable Development) to summarize the key points raised during the debate; the summary will be passed on to the drafting group of the Bonn Declaration to be adopted at the end of the conference. The chairs will then formally close the Segment.

Working languages

The Conference plenary sessions as well as the High-level Segment will be interpreted in English, French, Spanish, German and Arabic. Interpretation in Chinese will be provided for the first Conference day.

Workshop and project-based workshops will be interpreted in English and French. All Conference documents will be made available in English and French.

Reporting process

The reporting process should be carried out by the following persons nominated by the Conference Task Force:

General rapporteurs

- Mary Joy Pigozzi (AED), member of DESD High-level Panel; [rapporteur for plenary sessions, high-level segment, etc.)
- Kartikeya Sarabhai (Director GEE India); [rapporteur for workshops]

Thematic cluster rapporteurs

- "Relevance of ESD for key Sustainable development challenges": Hilligje van 't Land (The Netherlands)

- "Building partnerships to promote ESD"): Overson Shumba (Zambia); MEEG
- "Capacity Development for ESD": Konai Thaman (Fiji); IAG
- "ESD and the teaching-learning process": Miriam Vilela (Brazil/Costa Rica); Reference Group]

Moreover, each workshop will have its own rapporteur nominated by the workshop coordinators.

The two general rapporteurs of the conference are responsible for reporting on conference results in the mid-conference and the closing plenaries. The general rapporteur responsible for the workshops receives input from four thematic cluster rapporteurs. The four thematic cluster rapporteurs receive input from the rapporteurs of each workshop. Additional input for the thematic cluster rapporteurs is provided by rapporteurs of the project-based workshops. Each rapporteur should structure their report along the four conference objective. Workshop rapporteurs must use for their reporting a specific template that is structured along the four conference objectives.

A comprehensive report of the Conference will be produced and made available to participants and the wider public via the Conference website, the UNESCO website and other channels before end-2009.

Drafting Process for Bonn Declaration

A drafting group will be responsible for drafting the Bonn Declaration. It consists of a core of ESD experts and experienced drafters, the general rapporteurs, the thematic cluster rapporteurs of the conference, a senior representative of the UNESCO Education Sector and representatives of UNESCO's electoral groups.

Composition of drafting group (30 members):

Chairperson (1)

- Charles Hopkins (Canada, IAG)

Drafting Secretariat (3)

- Heila Lotz-Sisitka (South Africa, IAG)
- Roland Bernecker (German Natcom)
- Jean-Yves Le Saux (UNESCO)

General rapporteurs (2) (See above)

Thematic cluster rapporteurs (4) (See above)

UNESCO Education Sector (1)

- Nicholas Burnett (or Ana Luiza Machado)

Japanese expert (1)

- Mr. Yoshihiro Natori

Representatives of UNESCO Electoral Groups (18: 3 per group)

Input for the drafting group will be provided, among others, by the two general rapporteurs of the conference: one for the workshops, one for the plenary sessions, the high-level segment and other conference elements. The general rapporteur responsible for the workshops receives input from four thematic cluster rapporteurs, who in turn receive input from the rapporteurs of each workshop.

Further input for the consideration of the Bonn Declaration drafting group will come from the summaries of pre-meetings in the lead-up to the Bonn Conference (e.g., Bordeaux International Conference on ESD, 27-29 October 2008; Gothenburg Conference on ESD "Visions and preparations for a common blueprint on ESD", 11-12 November 2008; MESA International Conference "Environment, Development and Climate Change: Universities Responding?", 24-28 November 2008; Tokyo International Forum on ESD Dialogue, 3-5 December 2008); documents such as the Basic Information Document of the Bonn Conference, the International Implementation Scheme (2005) and the Ahmedabad Declaration (2007); and the Draft Global Report on Context and Structures of the Work on ESD (available via the Conference website) and the associated summary of findings.

The drafting group is expected to prepare a draft preamble and agree on a structure of the Declaration in advance of the conference.

The general, cluster and workshop rapporteurs will also provide input for the conference proceedings to be published after the conference.

Drafting group meetings at Bonn

The first face-to-face meeting of the entire drafting group will take place in Bonn in the afternoon of Monday 30 March 2009. As a result of this meeting, the drafting secretariat will be called upon to prepare a 'zero draft' of the Bonn Declaration for sharing with the drafting group the following day (Day 1 of the conference). The 'zero draft' and subsequent drafts of the Bonn Declaration will be available in two languages only—English and French.

The three-member drafting secretariat will be expected to meet regularly throughout the conference; its first meeting should take place on the morning of Monday 30 March.

The full drafting group is expected to meet at the following moments during the conference:

Day 1 (Tuesday 31 March): at breakfast (to review the 'zero draft') and in the early evening, when the first inputs from the conference will be considered. The drafting secretariat will then work on producing the first draft.

Day 2 (Wednesday 1 April): at breakfast (to review and approve the firsf *draft,* which will be distributed to all conference participants that morning with a view to receiving feedback by 15.30); and in the late afternoon/early evening in order to prepare the second draft that will be shared with all conference participants that evening, taking account of feedback and results of workshops and plenary sessions.

Day 3 (Thursday 2 April): Late morning/lunch time in order to review the feedback received on the second draft (by 11.00 a.m.) and to consider inputs from the workshop sessions taking place in the morning of Day 3.

The full drafting group may also meet on other occasions during the conference, as may be considered necessary by its chairperson.

No interpretation will be available for the meetings of the drafting group.

Availability of draft Bonn Declaration

The first draft of the Bonn Declaration will be made available to all participants in the morning of Day 2; feedback (either consolidated, as may occur in the case of the electoral groups, or individual) should be received by 1530 hours that afternoon, deposited at the conference secretariat.

The second draft will be made available in the evening of Day 2 (upon return from project-based workshops at the arrival point of the buses) and at breakfast of Day 3. Feedback should be received no later than 1100 on the morning of Day 3, deposited at the conference secretariat.

The third draft will be made available at 1430 (30 minutes before the start of the closing plenary) on Day 3.

The final draft will be that agreed by the conference participants in the closing plenary session of the conference (chaired by Ricardo Henriques, former Vice-Minister of Education, Brazil). It will be adopted by consensus.

CHAPTER

Welcome by Koïchiro Matsuura, Director-General of UNESCO

delivered by Nicholas Burnett
Assistant Director-General for Education, UNESCO

Federal Minister of Education and Research of Germany,
Honourable President of the Standing Conference of the Ministers of Education and Culture of the German Länder, Ms Grace Machel,
Ministers,
Heads of Delegation,
Ladies and Gentlemen,

It is a great pleasure and honour for me to open this mid-term review conference for the UN Decade of Education for Sustainable Development. I warmly thank the Government of Germany for its generosity in hosting this World Conference and providing such a splendid venue in Bonn. My particular thanks to Minister Schavan for all of her efforts to ensure the success of this important event.

We are deeply honoured by the presence of Ms Graca Machel, an outstanding woman of Africa who has stood up for the rights and needs of children everywhere. We are very much looking forward to your keynote presentation and to the distinctive perspective you bring to the themes of this conference.

I also look forward to the remarks of Queen Rania of Jordan who, for reasons beyond her control, is unable to join us in person this morning. I know she is greatly disappointed not to be here in Bonn, but through the video that will be shown, I am sure that her thoughts on the global picture of education will be inspiring to us all.

Let me take this opportunity to welcome all of you: namely, the over 900 participants who have come to this conference from all regions, all sectors and all constituencies of the Decade. Among you are some fifty ministers or deputy ministers of education and representatives of more than 100 countries. This is a clear sign that the theme of this conference—education for sustainable development (ESD)—is rising higher on national agendas. I am confident that, with your participation and engagement, this World Conference will be a real milestone not only within the Decade but also for the success of ESD in the longer term.

This World Conference is, of course, highly important in its own right. But it is also part of a series of major international education events that UNESCO is holding in 2008-2009 focused—beyond ESD—on inclusive education, basic education for all, adult learning, and higher education.

This conference cycle aims to encourage a dynamic and far-reaching reflection on the transformative power of education. It also seeks to engage policy-makers, researchers, practitioners and a range of institutions in re-orienting education systems—from pre-school to adult learning, in formal and non-formal settings—in ways that promote equity, innovation and sustainable development—Nicholas Burnett.

Excellencies, Ladies and Gentlemen,

In a world trying to come to grips with a major financial and economic crisis, with environmental degradation and climate change, with social tensions and conflict, there is growing global consensus that the international community must unite to prepare for a better common future. This consensus was anticipated by the decision of the UN General Assembly to create a Decade of Education for Sustainable Development (DESD), running from 2005 to 2014, in recognition of the critical role that education plays in development.

But it is not just any kind of education. It is about learning for change and about learning to change. In particular, it is about the content and processes of education that will help us to learn to live together sustainably. If education systems are characterized by inequality, discrimination and exclusion, they risk perpetuating or even deepening the social and economic disparities that exist. That is why ESD aims to encourage a shift towards more inclusive education systems, grounded in a respect for diversity and a recognition of interdependence—both with each other and the environment in which we live. ESD is based on the belief that everyone has the right to learn, the capacity to contribute and the commitment to ensure that others share in the benefits of development. This belief is also at the heart of the Education for All goals and indeed the entire Millennium Development agenda.

The strategies UNESCO is putting in place, as global coordinator of the EFA movement and of the DESD, are aimed at linking quality education for all with the ultimate goal of sustainable development in each and every country. Yet, this goal is under tremendous pressure. There is a widespread sense that time is running out, that key decisions are being deferred and delayed, and that public opinion remains poorly informed about what is at stake.

All of us—individuals, organizations, Governments—have difficult choices to make. ESD is a way to make those choices better informed, more attuned to the urgency of the problems we face, and more aligned with the core human values that bind us together. And let us never forget that our choices today are not just for ourselves but also for the future—in other words, for our children, our grandchildren and their descendants. In a sense, of course, we no longer have a choice. The principles, values and practices of sustainable development must find their place in children's schooling, higher education, community-based learning activities and workplace training programmes. If the aim of ESD is to provide us with the knowledge, skills and competences to address the problems that we face in the 21st century, then ESD is not an option but an imperative.

To be relevant and up-to-date, ESD must engage seriously with today's issues and challenges. Take the case of climate change, which as you know will be the subject of a major UN conference in Copenhagen in December 2009. While climate change is not the only environmental threat to the sustainability of the planet, it is a priority for policy-makers and the general public alike because it will affect all of us. Education for and about climate change is a significant aspect of ESD; and the ESD perspective—with its emphasis on the economic, the social and the cultural as well as the environmental dimensions—can be especially helpful in shaping our response. With support from the Government of Denmark. UNESCO will be organizing an international seminar on climate change education in Paris in late July. This meeting will learn from the discussions here in Bonn and will provide a valuable educational perspective for the Copenhagen conference in December.

Excellencies, Ladies and Gentlemen,

We are gathered here in Bonn to reflect on how we can move forward the ESD agenda. In this regard, it is vital that we build on the lessons of experience. The DESD Global Monitoring and Evaluation Framework was put in place to assess the implementation of the Decade. This week we are making available the latest draft of the global report on DESD implementation, which focuses on the structures and mechanisms put into place to advance all of our work on ESD at global, regional and national levels. In addition, in the lead-up to Bonn, a number of meetings took place—in Bordeaux,

Gothenburg, Nairobi and Tokyo—whose outcomes will likewise feed into our discussions.

Let me highlight three of the lessons or findings that I find particularly valuable.

First, there is the importance of partnership. No single body—not UNESCO, not the whole UN system—can do ESD on its own. Closely linked to the idea of sustainability is the concept of inter-dependence, which demands that we work together to overcome shared problems. We must act quickly and that means we must partner together quickly too. We sometimes talk loosely of 'multi-stakeholder partnerships' but ESD is one of those areas where such partnerships are essential. We know that, together, we can actually do something in and through education in order to create a safer and more sustainabJe world. UNESCO has always emphasized the important role civil society has to play in mobilizing enthusiasm and commitment for BSD, and appreciates the valuable contribution of the Earth Charter initiative.

Second, there is the key role of teachers and educators, who are the cornerstone of effective ESD programmes. There are over 60 million teachers in the world today and countless numbers of non-formal educators. They work at the 'local' level but are called upon to deal with 'global' issues. To make education relevant and real to learners, they must draw upon local inputs, contexts and values. Hence, we need to remember that teachers are individuals, part of educational and learning institutions, part of a community, and part of a society, and that they need to be supported in their work.

Third, it is vital to understand that the ESD approach is not limited to particular topics or even curriculum content in general, but offers a larger vision of what are the purpose and objectives of education, what is the relevance of education, what is the environment within which learning takes place, what kinds of values and principles are imparted and what types of skills, competences, behaviours and attitudes are generated. ESD has something important to say to all of these considerations, which coalesce around the question of quality.

We recognize that the 'education' in ESD is not just formal schooling but embraces a wide range of learning experiences and programmes. The focus on basic education and literacy in the orientation of the Decade is important. Yet BSD must also inform secondary education, technical and vocational training, and higher education, and a wide range of other modalities of learning that may be labelled as non-formal education, professional development and training.

We believe that such an inclusive approach serves as a stimulus to improving the quality of education. That is:

- an education that is relevant to the key challenges of living in the twenty-first century;
- an education that empowers people to exercise their rights while also builds a stronger sense of responsibility;
- an education that ensures that a person is educated to think critically, to solve problems, to work in teams, to be analytical, to be confident about facing situations of ambiguity and difficulty in the workplace or in their lives; and *finally*,
- an education that cultivates good citizenship locally, nationally and globally. ESD can contribute to this quality agenda in many important ways.

Excellencies, Ladies and Gentlemen,

The UN Decade on Education for Sustainable Development is a framework for partnership and collaboration, bringing together a great diversity of interests and concerns. It is an instrument of mobilization and advocacy, through which governments, international organizations, civil society, the private sector and local communities around the world can demonstrate their practical commitment to learning to live sustainably. Thus, ESD has come to be seen as a process of learning how to make decisions that consider the long-term future of the economy, ecology and the equitable development of all communities. Building the capacity for such future-oriented thinking is a key task of education.

As facilitator of this Decade, UNESCO is assisting countries and regions develop educational plans and strategies that are relevant to their different realities and concerns. But no country is an island when it comes to sustainable development. In this regard, even islands are not islands! We do live in a truly interdependent world and an educational experience that ignores or denies this cannot prepare citizens for the reality of living on this small planet.

In conclusion, I would like to stress that each of us is an agent of change and that we can individually and together contribute to creating a better world. All of us have responsibility, whether at the local, national, regional or international level, for the implementation of the Decade. But I do not wish to make this duty sound like a burden because it is quite the reverse—it is a way to express our creativity and our capacity for innovation as well as to enjoy working and living with others in common cause.

Let me once again express my gratitude to Germany for providing us with such a warm welcome and hospitality. I would also like to thank Japan for its offer to host the wrap-up meeting for the Decade in 2014. This is a very timely proposal from a country that was the prime mover behind the creation of the DESD.

It remains for me to express my hope that this conference fulfils its promise by providing a rich and rewarding experience to every participant and by convincing all of you—if you need to be convinced that the Decade of Education for Sustainable Development is a key framework for cooperation to achieve a better, more sustainable and safer world.

Thank you.

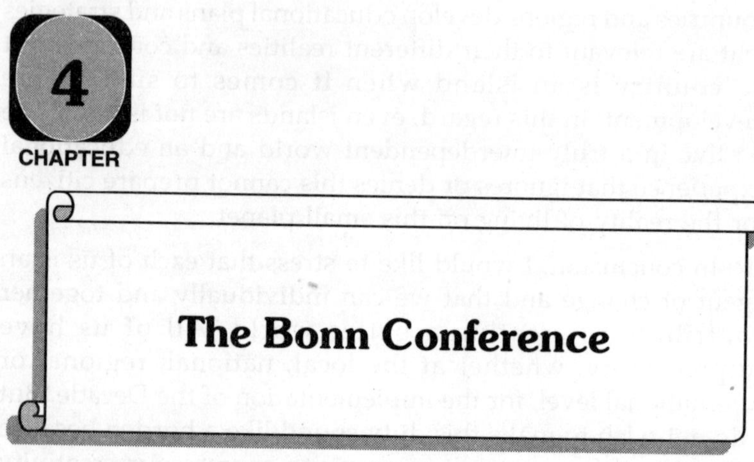

The Bonn Conference

This document provides basic information about the UNESCO World Conference on Education for Sustainable Development, to be held from 31 March to 2 April 2009 in Bonn, Germany. It places the conference in the context of the UN Decade of Education for Sustainable Development (DESD, 2005-2014), explains the overall objectives, the programme elements and the expected outcomes of the conference, and also provides a brief outline of the main themes and concerns of Education for Sustainable Development (ESD). The document was prepared in consultation with the International Advisory Group of the conference.

Sustainable Development

Sustainable development is one of the central challenges facing the world today. In the light of persisting global patterns of poverty and inequality, as highlighted by the MDG agenda, along with emerging issues like the impact of climate change and the current financial and economic crises, it is no exaggeration to say that, at the start of the 21st century, the world is at a major turning point. The definition of Sustainable development given by the World Commission on Environment and Development ('Brundtland Commission', 1987) remains valid and timely: "Sustainable development is development that meets the needs of the present without compromising the ability of future generations to meet their own needs." This implies a balance between and an integration of the environmental, economic and social aspects of development, with attention also paid to the cultural dimension. Sustainable development, in fact, has become the guiding principle for achieving just and equitable development options that benefit all people everywhere. Sustainable development can thus be understood both in time and space: it takes into account the needs of future generations, and equally the needs of people today in every part of the world.

Achieving Sustainable development requires a global change of mindset and behaviours. Indeed, it has long been recognized that education is crucial for achieving Sustainable development. The UN Conference on the Human Environment ('Stockholm Conference') in 1972 emphasized education as a way of addressing human-environment problems. Agenda 21, the document adopted at the UN Conference on Environment and Development (UNCED, 'Rio Summit', Rio de Janeiro, 1992), emphasized the need to promote education, public awareness and training in order to assist bringing about Sustainable development. In particular, Chapter 36 (Promoting education, public awareness and training) states: "*Education is critical for promoting Sustainable development and improving the capacity of the people to address environment and development issues.*"The World Summit on Sustainable Development (WSSD, Johannesburg, 2002) reaffirmed this commitment and recommended to the United Nations General Assembly the establishment of a United Nations Decade of Education for Sustainabie Development (DESD, 2005-2014), which clearly recognizes the increased need to integrate sustainable development issues and principles into education and learning. Thus, while education clearly is not a sufficient condition in itself for achieving sustainable development, it is certainly a necessary condition.

Education for Sustainable Development

Education for Sustainable Development (ESD) seeks to integrate the tenets, values and practices of sustainable development into all aspects of education and learning. ESD aims at providing every individual with the opportunity to acquire the values, competencies, knowledge and skills that enable him or her to contribute to a humane, socially just, economically viable and ecologically sustainable future. Among other things, ESD promotes a sense of both local and global responsibility, encourages future-oriented, anticipatory thinking, builds recognition of global interdependence and emphasizes cultural changes that embrace the values of sustainable development. Rather than remaining passive in the face of the above-mentioned challenges, ESD seeks to empower societies, communities and individuals everywhere to shape their future actively and responsibly. ESD raises interesting questions, for example, about learning how to generate creative solutions to current global challenges; about reflecting on new lifestyles which combine well-being, quality of life and respect for nature and other people; and about considering the viewpoints of people from different countries about what sustainability means in practice.

ESD is relevant not only to formal education settings, training and workplace learning but also to public awareness-raising and non-formal and informal learning of many kinds. Thus, ESD should not be seen narrowly as another subject or concern to be added onto the formal education system or a workplace training programme. Rather, ESD is a teaching and learning process through which understanding of and orientation towards sustainable development become embedded in the core education and learning processes to be found in societies everywhere.

In whatever setting, ESD encourages an interdisciplinary and holistic approach to teaching and learning and promotes critical and creative thinking in the educational process. It therefore implies new ways of teaching and learning. The aim of ESD—for individuals to act responsibly in a globalized world—must be integrated into the manner in which all learning occurs: life-long and life-wide, in the workplace, the home and throughout society in general. To holistically address the development of ESD initiatives, four main thrusts have been identified: access to quality education, the reorienting of existing education systems to address sustainability concerns, public awareness and understanding initiatives, and training programmes to address specific social, environmental and economic sustainability issues.

The UN Decade of Education for Sustainable Development

In December 2002, by Resolution 59/237, the UN General Assembly declared the years 2005-2014 the UN Decade of Education for Sustainable Development (DESD). Member States thus committed themselves to intensified efforts to integrate the principles, values and practices of Sustainable development into education and learning. The UN General Assembly designated UNESCO the lead agency for the global implementation and coordination of the DESD.

The International Implementation Scheme for the DESD (IIS, 2005), states: "The basic vision of the DESD is a world where everyone has the opportunity to benefit from education and learn the values, behaviour and lifestyles required for a Sustainable future and for positive societal transformation." The DESD should provide an opportunity for refining and promoting the vision of and transition to Sustainable development through all forms of education, public awareness and training. It should also help to give an enhanced profile to the important role of education and learning in promoting Sustainable development. In this context, the IIS proposes four main objectives for the DESD: to facilitate networking, linkages, exchange and interaction among stakeholders in ESD; to foster an increased quality of teaching and learning in ESD; to help countries make progress towards and attain the Millennium Development Goals through ESD efforts; and to provide countries with new opportunities to incorporate ESD into education reform efforts.

The complexity, breadth and diversity of Sustainable development issues and of ESD require that a wide range of stakeholders become active and come together to implement the DESD through a partnership approach: governments, parliaments, non-governmental organizations, media, the private sector, education institutions, research institutes, individual educators and students, among others. Bottom-up and top-down strategies must be combined. The local, national, regional and international levels are all relevant for a successful implementation of the DESD.

As global coordinator, UNESCO's role is to catalyze new partnerships; encourage monitoring and evaluation; facilitate the development of a research agenda for ESD; provide a forum for bringing together important stakeholders; share good practices; promote exchange between Member States on ESD; convene working groups on specific ESD topics; and provide strategic guidance.

Since the start of the DESD, many activities have been undertaken by a broad range of stakeholders. National Committees have been set up, networks have been established, education materials have been developed and disseminated, good practices have been highlighted and shared, and meetings have been organized to encourage international exchange. Much remains to be done, however, before ESD occupies a truly central place in educational and learning processes and before ESD fulfils its potential to improve the quality of education as a whole.

The DESD needs to be seen in conjunction with other international priorities in development and education. The Millennium Development Goals (MDGs) provide the relevant framework for international development cooperation; the six Education for All (EFA) goals aim at extending the reach of basic education to everyone; and the United Nations Literacy Decade (UNLD) focuses on the contribution of youth and adult literacy to building knowledge societies in which all may participate. With its orientation towards the principle of sustainable development, the DESD focuses specifically on the content and purpose of education and learning.

The World Conference on Education for Sustainable Development: Objectives, Themes and Expected Results

As the DESD approaches its mid-point, the "World Conference on Education for Sustainable Development—Moving into the Second Half of the UN Decade" will be held in Bonn, Germany, from 31 March to 2 April 2009, organized by UNESCO and the German Federal Ministry of Education and Research, in cooperation with the German Commission for UNESCO. The conference will provide a platform for dialogue and advocacy on ESD at the global level, involving some 700 participants from all regions representing UNESCO Member States, UN agencies, civil society organizations, youth and the private sector. The preparation of the conference is being carried out in consultation with an International Advisory Group.

The World Conference on ESD comes at a time when education is increasingly recognized as an important motor for change. It is ever more clear that a massive reorientation of the ways people all over the world think and act is required if a sustainable future is to be ensured. The conference will be a major opportunity to highlight the role ESD must play in this process.

Conference objectives

The World Conference on Education for Sustainable Development will pursue four main objectives:

1. To highlight the essential contribution of ESD to all of education and to achieving quality education —'Why is ESD relevant?'—

ESD, which is relevant to all types, levels and settings of education, is an approach to teaching and learning based on the ideals and principles that underlie sustainability. Since ESD engages with such key issues as human rights, poverty reduction, sustainable livelihoods, climate change, gender equality, corporate social responsibility, and the protection of indigenous cultures in an integral way, it constitutes a comprehensive approach to quality education and learning. By dealing with the problems faced by humanity in a globalized world, ESD will shape the purposes and content of all education in the period ahead; ESD is, indeed, education for the future. The World Conference will draw out the relevance of ESD to education as a whole and its importance for improving the quality of education while attaining Education for All (EFA) and the Millennium Development Goals. Moreover, it will seek ways to move ESD further from the margins into the centre of all education.

2. To promote international exchange on ESD —'What can we learn from each other?'—

All sustainable development programmes, including ESD, must consider the three spheres of sustainability—environment, society and economy, with culture as an underlying dimension. Because ESD addresses the local contexts of sustainability, it will take many forms around the world. The World Conference will provide an opportunity to share experiences, best practices and views on ESD from around the world. The question of how ESD can meet different regional, national and local as well as global needs will be addressed. Examples of good practice from all over the world will play an important role in identifying viable approaches to ESD.

3. *To carry out a stock-taking of DESD implementation —'What have we achieved so far, what are the lessons learnt?'—*

The empirical results as well as the global and regional reports from the first Monitoring and Evaluation exercise—currently being carried out by UNESCO—will provide input into discussions on the implementation of the DESD. The successes so far will be celebrated and presented while obstacles encountered and lessons learned will also be discussed.

4. *To develop strategies for the way ahead —'Where do we want to go from here?'—*

It is important that the analysis of implementation so far and the identification of past and emerging challenges and opportunities leads to the development of new strategies, ensuring the further implementation of the DESD in its second half. Strategies for the way forward may include, among others: the further integration of ESD in educational policies, plans and programmes; the mobilization of more resources for ESD; the establishment of effective partnerships (especially through North-South and South-South cooperation) and the inclusion of stakeholders not involved in implementing the DESD so far. Emerging sustainable development issues and the educational responses to them will also be discussed in this context.

Conference Thematic Clusters

In pursuing the four objectives, the workshops of the World Conference will focus on four thematic clusters. It is assumed that all four objectives will be addressed by each of the following four clusters. The following cross-cutting issues will be addressed in the workshops: Gender, Inclusion, Culture, Traditional Knowledge, Human Rights, UN Millennium Development Goals, Technology.

I—Relevance of ESP *for key sustainable development challenges*

ESD can contribute substantially to addressing key sustainable development challenges. Indeed, without reorienting education, successfully confronting issues like water and climate change, among many others, will not be possible. Moreover, introducing sustainable development issues into all areas of education will help to make education more relevant. Engaging students and learners in contemporary questions related to development brings education closer to life and enhances the learning experience by stimulating motivation and interest. The following workshops are foreseen for this thematic cluster:

	Workshop themes
1.	**Water** education and training for sustainable development
2.	Learning about **climate change** through ESD
3.	Advancing **sustainable lifestyles** and responsible consumption through ESD
4.	**ESD and risk management:** building resilient societies
5.	Educating for **food security:** the contribution of ESD
6.	AIDS, **Health** and Education for Sustainable Development
7.	Mainstreaming **Biodiversity** into education and learning
8.	**The economic pillar** of SD: educational approaches

II—Building partnerships to promote ESD

With sustainable development relating to all areas of society, reorienting education towards sustainable development must be a multi-stakeholder endeavour. Learning for sustainable development takes place not only in education institutions but also in many other sectors of society. Education stakeholders therefore need to reach out to other important actors and build strong partnerships. Because sustainable development is a global challenge, international partnerships and the integration of the local and the global are decisive elements for ESD as well. How strong partnerships for ESD can be built will be addressed in the following workshops:

	Workshop themes
9.	UNESCO **Biosphere Reserves** as learning sites for integrating local and global sustainability issues
10.	Delivering on CSR and **private sector** participation in the DESD
11.	Media as partners for ESD
12.	ESD in North-South-South & South-South partnerships and **development cooperation**

III—Capacity Development for ESD

If ESD is to become a central aspect of all education, supporting structures at the global, national and local levels are required. Among other things, this implies political frameworks that enable the inclusion of sustainable development issues and principles into all areas of teaching and learning. The active involvement of civil society is equally key to introducing a broad concept such as ESD into education. Finally, ESD implementation itself must be a learning experience. Monitoring and evaluating progress must therefore be an important concern for all stakeholders.

The following workshops will address capacities for the successful implementation of ESD:

	Workshop themes
13.	Global responsibilities and local realities to foster ESD through **institutional frameworks**
14.	The role of **Civil Society** in ESD
15.	From the margins into the centre: Establishing ESD in **education plans and curricula**
16.	**Teacher Education** to address sustainability
17.	**Monitoring and Evaluation of ESD**—Results and lessons learnt from the DESD M&E process and **indicators** for measuring progress in ESD

IV—ESD and the teaching-learning process

The integration of ESD into education varies among different fields of teaching and learning. Requirements, practices and opportunities of ESD vary from one education setting to another. Moreover, when addressing the role of ESD in education, the important question of how Education for All and ESD relate to each other must be considered. The main thrust of each workshop in this cluster is: how can ESD contribute to improving the quality of teaching-learning processes?

	Workshop themes
18.	Synergies and differences between **EFA and ESD** [Focus on Educational Quality and how ESD can contribute to Quality Education]
19.	Better schools at pre-school, primary and secondary levels through ESD [Focus on methodology, school environment, role of teachers, curriculum]
20.	The role of **HE and research** in ESD (teacher training, multidisciplinary research, innovation and critical reflection)
21.	ESD and lifelong learning
22.	ESD and **TVET**—developing skills and labour force competencies

Conference expected results

Among the expected results arising from the World Conference are the following:

- Strong impulse given to positioning ESD higher on the international education agenda.
- Better understanding of the essential contribution of ESD to quality education achieved.
- Further progress made towards acknowledging that ESD is an essential contribution to meeting sustainable development challenges at the local, national, regional and global levels.
- Good practices, experiences and views on ESD from all world regions exchanged in ways that will further enrich the implementation of the DESD.
- Substantial input gathered for the global mid-decade report on the DESD to be presented to the UNGA in 2010.
- Key strategic directions, priorities for action and partnership modalities identified for the second half of the DESD.

The main results of the conference, especially major recommendations, will be expressed in a Bonn Declaration. More detailed results (from plenaries, workshops and other conference processes) will be made available in a post-conference publication. It is envisaged that the Bonn Declaration will be submitted to the Executive Board and the General Conference of UNESCO for consideration with a view to strengthening UNESCO's role in the DESD and enhancing follow-up activities by Member States and other partners in the second half of the Decade.

Programme Elements of the World Conference

The World Conference programme will comprise the following elements:

In the *Opening Plenary*, the Director-General of UNESCO, Koïchiro Matsuura, and the German Federal Minister of Education and Research, Annette Schavan, will officially open the conference and introduce its objectives and themes. Keynote speakers will place the conference in the context of current education and sustainable development concerns and thus set the stage for the work to be undertaken during the three conference days.

Plenary Sessions will focus on the specific contributions of keynote speakers, the presentation and discussion of the Global Report on the DESD, and feedback from the workshops.

The Closing Plenary will consider the outcomes of the second set of workshops and draw together the conference's contribution to the four overall objectives with the help of rapporteurs. The Bonn Declaration on ESD will be adopted.

On the afternoon of the first day of the Conference (Tuesday, 31 March 2009), there will be a *ministerial High-Level Segment* on the theme of 'ESD and quality education', from 14.00 to 17.00. The session will be co-chaired by the Director-General of UNESCO, the Federal Minister of Education and Research of Germany (Ms Schavan) and the President of the KMK (Federal Office of the Lander in relation to Education).

A total of 22 *Workshops*—two sets of 11 parallel workshops—will address specific thematic and strategic issues with regard to ESD. They are grouped according to the four thematic clusters of the conference. The workshops will be organized and coordinated by key ESD experts and stakeholders, who are strongly encouraged to use an interactive format.

Project-Based Workshops, on the afternoon of the second conference day, will be held off-site and will provide participants with the opportunity to exchange views on best practice with the organizers of local ESD projects in the region and with one another. Project-based workshops will complement the on-site conference programme by providing 'hands-on' experiences of ESD. Each project-based workshop will have a specific thematic focus.

An ESD Projects Exhibition at the conference venue will present 25 concrete good practice projects selected from all over the world. Five projects per world region and representing different ESD approaches and stakeholders will be shown.

Special Events will address specific aspects and foci of ESD in addition to the conference workshops. Special events will be organized by individual ESD stakeholders—from governments, NGOs, the private sector, and so forth—and will be accredited by the conference organizers. They will take place during lunch hours or in the early evening in rooms at the conference centre and in surrounding institutions.

A number of *Associated Events* highlighting various aspects of ESD, mostly organized by local stakeholders, will take place before, during and after the conference in the city of Bonn.

The Member States and United Nations Agencies Exhibition Area will give UNESCO Member States and UN agencies the opportunity to present their activities in the context of the UN Decade of Education for Sustainable Development in an annex to the World Conference venue.

The organizers of the World Conference on ESD will also make sure that results of international meetings on ESD that take place in advance of the World Conference are taken into account in the preparation of the event. Results of previous meetings should be submitted to the organizers and should be structured along the four objectives of the World Conference. Preparation for the World Conference is an item on the agenda of the following meetings, among various others: International Conference on ESD, 27-29 October 2008, Bordeaux, France, organized by the French National Committee for the DESD within the framework of the French

Presidency of the Council of the European Union; International Workshop: Visions and Preparations for a Common Blueprint on ESD, 11-12 November 2008, Gothenburg, Sweden, organized by the Swedish Ministry of Education and Research, the Swedish Commission for UNESCO, Chalmers University and the University of Gothenburg; International Forum on ESD Dialogue, 2-5 December 2008, Tokyo, Japan, organized by the Ministry of Education, Culture, Sports, Science and Technology (MEXT) of Japan and the Japanese National Commission for UNESCO.

Key ESD Reference Documents

Framework for the UN DESD International Implementation Scheme

This reference document was prepared through consultation with other United Nations agencies, international organizations, governments, NGOs, universities, individuals and the private sector. It was presented at the 59th Session of the United Nations General Assembly (New York, September-October 2004). It served as the basis for the writing of the DESD International Implementation Scheme. English - http://unesdoc.unesco.org/images/0014/001486/148650E.pdf

DESD International Implementation Scheme

The DESD International Implementation Scheme was approved at the 172nd session of the UNESCO Executive Board.

English—http://unesdoc.unesco.org/images/0014/001486/148654E.pdf

United Nations Decade of Education for Sustainable Development (DESD 2005-2014): the first two years

English—http://unesdoc.unesco.org/images/0015/001540/154093e.pdf

Further documents will be made available on the conference website: ESDConference2009(5)unesco.org

CHAPTER

Bonn Declaration

Bonn Declaration

We, the *participants gathered at the UNESCO World Conference on Education for Sustainable Development held in Bonn, Germany on 31 March to 2 April 2009 issue the following statement and call for action:*

1. Despite unprecedented economic growth in the 20th century, persistent poverty and inequality still affect too many people, especially those who are most vulnerable. Conflicts continue to draw attention to the need for building a culture of peace. The global financial and economic crises highlights the risks of unsustainable economic development models and practices based on short-term gains. The food crisis and world hunger are an increasingly serious issue. Unsustainable production and consumption patterns are creating ecological impacts that compromise the options of current and future generations and the sustainability of life on Earth, as climate change is showing.

2. A decade into the 21st century, the world faces substantial, complex and interlinked development and lifestyle challenges and problems. The challenges arise from values that have created unsustainable societies. The challenges are interlinked, and their resolution requires stronger political commitment and decisive action. We have the knowledge, technology and skills available to turn the situation around. We now need to mobilise our potential to make use of all opportunities for improving action and change.
3. The impacts of unsustainable development, priorities, responsibilities and capacity differ between regions and between developing and developed countries. All countries will need to work collaboratively to ensure Sustainable development now and in the future. Investment in education for sustainable development (ESD) is an investment in the future, and can be a life-saving measure, especially in post-conflict and least developed countries.
4. Building on the Jomtien, Dakar and Johannesburg promises, we need a shared commitment to education that empowers people for change. Such education should be of a quality that provides the values, knowledge, skills and competencies for sustainable living and participation in society and decent work. The Education for All agenda underlines that the availability of basic education is critical for sustainable development. It similarly emphasises pre-school learning, education for rural people and adult literacy. Achievements in literacy and numeracy contribute to educational quality, and will also be critical to the success of ESD.
5. Through education and lifelong learning we can achieve lifestyles based on economic and social justice, food security, ecological integrity, sustainable livelihoods, respect for all life forms and strong values

that foster social cohesion, democracy and collective action. Gender equality, with special reference to the participation of women and girl children in education, is critical for enabling development and sustainability. Education for sustainable development is immediately necessary for securing sustainable life chances, aspirations and futures for young people.

Education for sustainable development in the 21st century

6. Education for sustainable development is setting a new direction for education and learning for all. It promotes quality education, and is inclusive of all people. It is based on values, principles and practices necessary to respond effectively to current and future challenges.
7. ESD helps societies to address different priorities and issues *inter alia* water, energy, climate change, disaster and risk reduction, loss of biodiversity, food crises, health risks, social vulnerability and insecurity. It is critical for the development of new economic thinking. ESD contributes to creating resilient, healthy and sustainable societies through a systemic and integrated approach. It brings new relevance, quality, meaning and purpose to education and training systems. It involves formal, non-formal and informal education contexts, and all sectors of society in a lifelong learning process.
8. ESD is based on values of justice, equity, tolerance, sufficiency and responsibility. It promotes gender equality, social cohesion and poverty reduction and emphasises care, integrity and honesty, as articulated in the Earth Charter. ESD is underpinned by principles that support sustainable living, democracy and human well-being. Environmental protection and restoration, natural resource conservation and sustainable use, addressing unsustainable production and consumption

patterns, and the creation of just and peaceful societies are also important principles underpinning ESD.

9. ESD emphasises creative and critical approaches, long-term thinking, innovation and empowerment for dealing with uncertainty, and for solving complex problems. ESD highlights the interdependence of environment, economy, society, and cultural diversity from local to global levels, and takes account of past, present and future.

10. Linked to different needs and the concrete living conditions of people, ESD provides the skills to find solutions and draws on practices and knowledge embedded in local cultures as well as in new ideas and technologies.

Progress in the UN Decade of Education for Sustainable Development

11. During the first five years of the UN Decade of Education for Sustainable Development, led and co-ordinated by UNESCO, many countries have made progress in implementing ESD and have designed innovative policy frameworks. A number of UN agencies, NGOs, regional bodies, and partner networks are engaged in concrete activities that support specific areas of ESD. Many people and organisations are committed and engaged in action. Efforts towards better understanding, promotion, implementation and assessment of the quality of ESD are underway. A global monitoring and evaluation framework has been designed. Efforts at the global level have been complemented by regional strategies and initiatives.

12. We recognise that education is a significant factor in improving human well-being. We now have the knowledge and experience available to significantly improve the contents, methods and purposes of

education. We know how to begin re-orienting education systems to emphasise lifelong learning. Through ESD we are learning how to improve links between formal, non-formal and informal education. We know the importance of strengthening and sharing knowledge of educational change processes.

13. Science has provided us with a better knowledge of climate change and of the Earth's life-support systems; it has gathered significant knowledge about HIV and AIDS, malaria, tuberculosis, heart diseases, and other serious health challenges. We know more about natural systems, and human impacts on them, and the ways that biodiversity supports our well-being. We know that current economic thinking has to change, and that there is a need to avoid unsustainable production and consumption and promote and support the emergence of 'sustainably developed' countries. Social science has provided insight into ethical, cultural, cognitive and affective aspects of human development, as well as sociologies of change.

14. We now need to put this knowledge into action. This is especially important to strengthen and extend the outcomes of the UN DESD in the next five years, but also to ensure longer term implementation of ESD.

A call for action

15. The progress of ESD remains unevenly distributed and requires different approaches in different contexts. In the coming years, there is a clear need for both developed and developing countries, civil society and international organisations to make significant efforts to:

At policy level in member states

(a) *Promote ESO's contribution to all of education and to achieving quality education,* with particular regard to fostering the linkages between ESD and EFA within a coherent and systemic approach. Foster the goals of the ESD agenda in international fora and at the national level.

(b) *Increase public awareness and understanding about sustainable development and ESD,* by mainstreaming and expanding the learning and insights gained in the first five years of the UN DESD into public awareness policies and programmes and various forms of informal learning. This should include promoting the role and contribution of *the media* for fostering public awareness and understanding of sustainability issues. It should also include capacity-building of media professionals.

(c) *Mobilize adequate resources and funding in favour of ESD,* in particular through integrating ESD into national development policy and budgetary frameworks, into UN common country programming processes and other country-level policy frameworks (such as sector-wide approaches), as well as into EFA and MDG initiatives. Promote and include ESD in the priorities of foundations and donors.

(d) *Re-orient education and training systems to address sustainability concerns through coherent policies at national and local levels.* Develop and implement ESD policies through co-ordinated inter-sectoral/inter-ministerial approaches that also involve business and the corporate sector, civil society, local communities and the scientific community.

(e) *Develop and strengthen existing international, regional and national enabling mechanisms and cooperation for ESD that respect cultural diversity.* Establish regional and country-level committees, networks and communities of practice for ESD that strengthen local-national, and national-global links, and that enhance *North-South-South and South-South co-operation.*

At practice level

(f) *Support the incorporation of sustainable development issues using an integrated and systemic approach in formal education as well as in non-formal and informal education at all levels,* in particular through the development of effective pedagogical approaches, teacher education, teaching practice, curricula, learning materials, and education leadership development, and also by recognizing-the significant contribution of non-formal education and informal learning as well as vocational and work-place learning. Sustainable development is a cross-cutting theme with relevance to all disciplines and sectors.

(g) *Reorient curriculum and teacher education programmes to integrate ESD into both pre-service and in-service programmes.* Support teacher education institutions, *teachers and professors* to network, develop, and research sound *pedagogical practice.* Specifically support teachers to develop ESD strategies that can work with large class sizes, and to evaluate ESD learning processes.

(h) Promote evidence-informed policy dialogue on ESD, drawing upon relevant *research, monitoring and evaluation strategies,* and the *sharing and recognition of good practices.* Develop national ESD indicators that inform the effective implementation and review of ESD outcomes and processes.

(i) *Develop and extend ESD partnerships to integrate ESD into training, vocational education and workplace learning* by involving civil society, public and private sectors, NGOs, and development partners.

ESD should become an integral part of the training of leaders in business, industry, trade union, non-profit and voluntary organizations, and the public services. Re-orient TVET programmes to include ESD.

(j) *Involve youth in the design and implementation of ESD.* Engage the commitment, solidarity and potential of youth and their organisations and networks in enhancing ESD. Foster young people's ownership of ESD questions and issues.

(k) *Enhance the major contribution and key role of civil society* in stimulating debate and public participation, and initiating ESD actions. Explore ways to further this involvement and commitment.

(l) *Value and give due recognition to the important contribution of traditional, indigenous and local knowledge systems for ESD* and value different cultural contributions in promoting ESD.

(m) ESD should actively promote *gender equality,* as well as create conditions and strategies that enable women to share knowledge and experience of bringing about social change and human well-being.

(n) *Develop knowledge through ESD networking.* Identify and support schools, universities and other higher education and research institutions, education centres and education networks that could serve as centres of expertise and innovation that develop and share knowledge, and create resources for ESD. Explore the potential of specific geographical and bioregional sites which can serve as spatially defined 'laboratories' for ESD.

(o) Encourage and enhance *scientific excellence, research and new knowledge development* for ESD through the *involvement of higher education institutions and research networks* in ESD. Mobilise the core functions of universities: teaching, research and community engagement to strengthen global and local knowledge of ESD, and utilise the UNESCO ESD Chairs and UNESCO programme networks in this process. Establish institutional and organisational structures that facilitate flexibility, student participation, and multi-disciplinary programmes and develop model projects that can respond to the complexity and urgency of ESD. Reward structures should be developed and implemented to support ESD initiatives and research in higher education.

(p) *Develop institutional mechanisms* during the UN Decade of Education for Sustainable Development and other ongoing Decades, such as the UN Decade for Action 'Water for Life' that will ensure that ESD continues to be implemented beyond those Decades.

(q) *Engage the expertise available within the UN system* to strengthen ESD in key sustainable development conventions; for example, those focusing on biodiversity, climate change, desertification and intangible cultural heritage.

(r) *Intensify efforts in education and training systems to address critical and urgent sustainability challenges* such as climate change, water and food security by developing specific action plans and/or programmes within the UN DESD umbrella and partnership framework.

16. The participants in the 2009 World ESD Conference request UNESCO, as lead agency responsible for the UN DESD, to:

(a) Enhance its leadership and co-ordination role for the UN DESD based on the International Implementation

Scheme in co-operation with other UN agencies and programmes such as UNEP, UNU, the EFA convening agencies (UNICEF, UNDP, UNFPA and the World Bank)—amongst others, and incorporate ESD into 'one UN' strategies at country level, particularly through UNDAF processes.

(b) Support member states and other partners in the implementation of the UN DESD, particularly through upstream capacity-building and policy advice on the development of coherent national strategies, monitoring and evaluation, recognising and sharing good practices on ESD, advocacy and global partnership development, with due consideration to post-conflict and least developed countries.

(c) Represent and/or promote the ESD agenda in other major education and development forums such as international conferences and negotiations such as the G8, G20, Copenhagen Climate Change Conference, EFA High-level Group, UN Chief Executives Board, and UNESCO world conferences (amongst other ongoing events and activities).

(d) Utilize the expertise that exists within UNESCO biosphere reserves, world heritage sites and other science, culture and education programmes, such as TTISSA (Teacher Training Initiative for Sub-Saharan Africa), ASPnet schools and LIFE (Literacy Initiative for Empowerment) to further ESD objectives and ensure that key priorities for ESD are integrated into longer term programmes and strategies within UNESCO.

(e) Promote ESD-related research through UNESCO's programmes in order to enhance the quality and evidence-base of ESD. Further develop the global monitoring and evaluation system to evaluate ESD and take initiatives to develop international strategies and practices that can lead to a successful conclusion of the UN DESD with visible and concrete outcomes.

(f) Highlight the relevance and importance of education and training in the UN Summit on Climate Change (COP 15) in Copenhagen, Denmark, in December 2009 in consultation and co-operation with other partners.

(g) Intensify efforts and initiatives to put climate change education higher on the international agenda, in the framework of the DESD, in the context of UNESCO's strategy for action on climate change, and as a component of UN-wide action.

Furthermore, the participants in this conference undertake to work towards implementation of this Declaration.

The participants encourage the mobilization of adequate funding in support of the recommendations contained in this Declaration.

The participants in the World ESD Conference express their gratitude to the German government for hosting this conference, and welcome the intention announced by the Government of Japan to host jointly with UNESCO the end-of-decade world conference on ESD.

CHAPTER

Report by the Director-General on the UNESCO World Conference on ESD and the Bonn Declaration

Summary

In pursuance of 177 EX/Decision 9 and 34 C/Resolution 19, this report was prepared to provide information on the UNESCO World Conference on "Education for Sustainable Development—Moving into the Second Half of the United Nations Decade" (31 March-2 April 2009, Bonn, Germany, organized by UNESCO and the German Federal Ministry of Education and Research in cooperation with the German Commission for UNESCO) and the Bonn Declaration.

1. The UNESCO World Conference on "Education for Sustainable Development—Moving into the Second Half of the United Nations Decade" brought together 900 participants (53% male and 47% female), drawn from 147 countries. One hundred and twenty-three of UNESCO's Member States (including three Associate Members) were officially represented. The Conference aimed to:

(*a*) highlight the essential contribution of Education for Sustainable Development (ESD) to all of education and to achieving quality education ('Why is ESD relevant?'). Indeed, ESD, which is relevant to all types, levels and settings of education, is an approach to teaching and learning based on the ideals and principles that underlie sustainability. Since ESD engages with such key issues as human rights, poverty reduction, Sustainable livelihoods, climate change, gender equality, corporate social responsibility and protection of indigenous cultures in an integral way, it constitutes a comprehensive approach to quality education and learning. By dealing with the problems faced by humanity in a globalized world, ESD will shape the purposes and content of all education in the period ahead—ESD is, indeed, education for the future;

(*b*) promote international exchange on ESD ('What can we learn from each other?'). All Sustainable development programmes, including ESD, must consider the three spheres of sustainability—environment, society and economy, with culture as an underlying dimension. As ESD addresses the local contexts of sustainability, it will take many forms around the world. The sharing of best practices and different experiences and perspectives is vital for identifying key needs and for designing viable approaches to ESD;

(*c*) carry out a stock-taking of DESD implementation ('What have we achieved so far, what are the lessons learnt?'). The empirical results as well as the global and regional reports from the first Monitoring and Evaluation exercise - carried out by UNESCO -provided input into discussions on the implementation of the Decade. The successes to date were celebrated and presented, while the obstacles encountered and lessons learnt were also discussed; and (*d*) develop strategies for the way ahead ("Where do we want to go from here?"). It is important that the analysis of implementation to date and identification of past and emerging challenges and opportunities lead to the development of new strategies for the second half of the Decade. These may include, among others, the further integration of ESD in educational policies, plans and programmes; the mobilization of more resources for ESD; the establishment of effective partnerships (especially through North-South and South-South cooperation); and the inclusion of stakeholders not involved in implementing the Decade to date. Emerging sustainable development issues and the educational responses to them were discussed in this context.

2. The opening session helped to frame the context of the Conference and set the tone for ensuing discussions and subsequent sessions. This was done through several keynote addresses, including a video message from Queen Rania of Jordan and an inspirational speech by Ms Graca Machel, who reminded participants of the need to keep the promises made in Jomtien and Dakar regarding education and sustainable human development.

3. Plenary sessions provided opportunities for all participants to be introduced to and discuss various issues. In particular, one plenary session was focused on the DESD Monitoring and Evaluation process, with a presentation of the key findings of the draft global report on the context and structures of ESD, as well as regional perspectives. The final plenary session was the occasion for all participants to adopt the Bonn Declaration.

4. A high-level segment gave 47 ministers and deputy-ministers of education the opportunity to discuss achievements in their respective countries and the way ahead regarding implementation of the DESD, especially in the perspective of ESD's contribution to quality education. This

session stressed that ESD is one of the key drivers towards sustainability, the need to accelerate actions in the second half of the Decade, and the urgency of moving towards more sustainable practices.

5. Twenty-two workshops addressed specific thematic and strategic issues with regard to ESD. They were grouped according to the four thematic clusters of the conference, which were: relevance of ESD for key sustainable development challenges; building partnerships to promote ESD; capacity development for ESD; and ESD and the teaching-learning process.

6. Project-based workshops were held in and around Bonn, and provided participants with the opportunity to exchange views on best practice with the organizers of local ESD projects in the region and with one another. The project-based workshops complemented the on-site conference programme by providing 'hands-on' experiences of ESD.

7. An ESD Projects Exhibition at the conference venue presented 25 concrete good practice projects selected from all over the world. Five projects per world region, representing different ESD approaches and stakeholders, were on display.

8. The day before the World Conference, a workshop on "Young ESD Voices from around the World" brought together 25 young people from different parts of the world who have demonstrated engagement in ESD. Workshop participants discussed ESD in their respective countries and looked at what should be the main emphases for the second half of the DESD, as well as what their joint and individual engagement towards implementing the DESD in its second half could be. Workshop results were presented at the Opening Plenary of the Conference. The youth workshop participants then took part in the Conference.

9. The Conference website (www.esd-world-conference-2009.org/) can be consulted for further information on the different conference sessions. The final report of the Bonn

Conference will be made available in time for the 2009 UNESCO General Conference.

The Bonn Declaration

10. The Bonn Declaration reflects the discussions held during the Conference and provides a strategic orientation for the second half of the Decade. It attests the importance of ESD in the current world situation. It calls for making a compact with the global DESD movement aimcd at improving knowledge, skills and competencies and strengthening values and attitudes oriented towards a transition to a more just, fair and viable world.

11.. The Bonn Declaration was drafted through a transparent, inclusive, participatory and results-oriented approach to ensure its relevance for ESD and the Decade. In particular, in light of the present context of financial and economic crises and global challenges, it places emphasis on several key areas, which include: reinforcing the educational response to sustainable development challenges; developing and building capacities for adapting to change; sharing knowledge and experiences; and reinforcing synergies between different education and development initiatives.

12. The Bonn Declaration will serve as the backbone for the development of the post-Bonn process within the framework of the DESD. It is to be noted that the participants in the Bonn Conference welcomed the offer announced by the Government of Japan to host the end-of-decade world conference on ESD, which would be jointly organized by UNESCO and the Government of Japan. The full Bonn Declaration can be found in the Annex of this document.

Moving into the second half of the Decade: towards a strategic roadmap for the DESD

13. The pre-Bonn events leading up to the World Conference, the findings from the DESD Global Monitoring and Evaluation

Framework regarding the context and structure of work on ESD, discussions during the various sessions of the Bonn Conference itself and the Bonn Declaration highlighted key strategic areas of focus to put knowledge into action and promote further progress in ESD during the next five years:

- addressing global challenges through ESD;
- developing capacities;
- further re-orienting education and training to address sustainability concerns;
- building and sharing knowledge, as well as generating new knowledge through research;
- advocating for ESD, and increasing awareness and understanding of sustainability;
- reinforcing/enhancing synergies between different education and development initiatives; and
- extending and strengthening ESD partnerships.

14. UNESCO, with the help of the DESD Reference Group, the Monitoring and Evaluation Expert Group, the International Advisory Group for the World Conference, and the United Nations Inter-Agency Committee for the DESD, has already started to design a multi-stakeholder consultative process to develop a strategic roadmap for the second half of the Decade. This roadmap will seek to ensure ownership and commitment on the part of member States and key stakeholder groups for an accelerated implementation of the rest of the DESD. The preparation of this roadmap will involve, among other considerations, updating aspects of the International Implementation Scheme in light of the recommendations from the Bonn Conference.

15. The post-Bonn process will build on the discussions and lessons from the Bonn Conference. The DESD concerns all stakeholders, who can contribute to the success of the Decade and be agents of change at their own level, in their own communities and nations. As it is a United Nations

Decade, all United Nations agencies must be mobilized behind and engage with the Decade. UNESCO has to enhance* its leadership and coordination role, in cooperation with all stakeholders. Member States must be in the driver's seat for ensuring the implementation of the DESD at national level. UNESCO, as lead agency of the DESD, is committed to continue mobilizing stakeholders around ESD and to lead this global movement to a successful completion of the Decade.

16. The process of putting together this strategic roadmap will involve multi-stakeholder consultations through various mediums, including at upcoming conferences (such as CONFINTEA VI and the World Conference on Higher Education) and other events, as well as through electronic means. A first outline of the post-Bonn process and strategic roadmap will be presented to the 182nd session of the Executive Board in the autumn of 2009.

17. The fully-fledged strategic roadmap for the second half of the DESD will be presented along with the mid-term progress report on the implementation of the Decade (as requested by United Nations General Assembly resolution 59/237) to the United Nations General Assembly at its sixty-fifth session in the autumn of 2010.

18. UNESCO, together with the conference participants, would like to express its sincere thanks to the Government of Germany for their generosity in co-organizing and hosting the UNESCO World Conference on Education for Sustainable Development in Bonn.

PART—II
WORKSHOPS

CHAPTER

Workshop—1

Education for Water Sustainability *Where Decades Meet*

Background

Lack of appropriate institutional and human capacities, including education and training, have been systematically identified as one of the main barriers for the sustainable management of freshwater resources and for the achievement of the water-related Millennium Development Goals. To strengthen the capacities of Member States in water and education, the international community has designated two time periods focussing specifically on these issues, namely the United Nations Decade of Education for Sustainable Development (UN DESD, 2005-2014) and the International Decade for Action 'Water for Life' (2005-2015). Having as a main objective assessing the current status of water education and identifying the way forward as part of the process initiated during the 6th phase of the International Hydrological Programme (IHP), the workshop on "Education for Water Sustainability: Where Decades meet" during the UNESCO World Conference on Education for Sustainable

Development, ESD 2009 in Bonn, Germany, will also demonstrate and strengthen the links between UN and International decades working on water education.

Many United Nations bodies and Member States, including Germany, have substantially contributed to the ongoing UN DESD and to the International Decade for Action 'Water for Life', as well as to the programmes of the inter-agency mechanism UN-Water, including the UN-Water Decade on Capacity Development (UNW-DPC) and its water-related capacity development carried out to support the water decade. The background includes, among others:

- The International Conference on Freshwater, organised in Bonn in 2001 (www.water-2001.de) as part of the preparations for the 2002 World Summit on Sustainable Development (WSSD). The findings of the conference are summarised in the five so-called Bonn Keys:
    1. meeting the water security needs of the poor;
    2. decentralisation: the local level is where national policy meets community needs;
    3. better water outreach through new partnerships;
    4. long-term harmony with nature and neighbour through cooperative arrangements at the water basin level;
    5. stronger, better performing governance arrangements.

  Of the 27 recommendations for action agreed on, four explicitly concerned capacity development:

  18—Focus education and training on water wisdom, 19—Focus research and information management on problem solving, 20—Make water institutions more effective, 21—Share knowledge and innovative technologies.

  Also at the Bonn conference water was acknowledged as a key to sustainable development.

- The World Summit on Sustainable Development (WSSD) held in 2002 in Johannesburg, South Africa, which also focussed on the targets of the Millennium Development Goals (MDGs) specifically addressing water and sanitation issues. The outcome of the 2001 Bonn Freshwater Conference had helped to strengthen this link between the MDGs and water.

  In Johannesburg also a basis was laid for the United Nations Decade of Education for Sustainable Development. The Johannesburg Plan of Implementation underpinned the overall importance of water for sustainable development, and asked the member states to prepare national plans for the implementation of Integrated Water Resources Management by the end of 2005.

- In 2002 the United Nations General Assembly adopted a resolution proclaiming the United Nations Decade of Education for Sustainable Development (UN DESD), 2005-2014. The United Nations Educational, Scientific and Cultural Organization is the lead agency for the promotion of the Decade; the thematic programme on education for sustainable water management is led by UNESCO's International Hydrological Programme. Moreover, the UN General Assembly, in 2003, proclaimed the years 2005 to 2015 as the International Decade for Action 'Water for Life'. Also in 2003, UN-Water was endorsed as the official UN mechanism for the follow-up of the water-related decisions reached at the 2002 WSSD and the MDGs. UN-Water is also coordinating the International Decade for Action 'Water for Life'. In 2006 Germany offered to financially support the efforts of UN-Water by hosting one of the UN-Water Programme offices, the UN-Water Decade Programme on Capacity Development (UNW-DPC) in Bonn, Germany.

Workshop

Objective

This water and education related workshop will contribute to the overall objectives of the conference, particularly by:

- Highlighting the essential contributions of education for water sustainability to all education and to achieving quality education. ("Why are water and education relevant for sustainable development?").
- Carrying out a stock-taking of DESD implementation ("What have we achieved so far, what are the lessons learnt?").

  In preparation of the workshop existing water education approaches developed under the auspices of the two decades were identified (stock-taking e.g. via the regional workshops on water education organized by UNESCO-IMP and partners and by a short scrutiny of UN and national focal points). The workshop will include reports on outcomes from regional workshops, national programmes of Member States, examples from NGO programmes, among others.
- Promoting international exchange between water and education stakeholders, and in particular between the UN DESD and the International Decade for Action 'Water for Life' ('What can we learn from each other?').

The workshop will also demonstrate and strengthen the links between the two decades; i.e. the United Nations Decade of Education for Sustainable Development and the International Decade for Action 'Water for Life' as regards their contribution to achieving quality education for sustainable development.

The workshop will facilitate the exchange of ideas and of education approaches aimed at improving different levels of education.

The specific focus of the workshop on 'Education for Water Sustainability' is to identify opportunities and develop new concepts for the way ahead for water and education, including for the national, regional and international bodies in charge of the water and education decades ('Where do we want to go from here?').

This includes developing strategies for promoting capacity development in different levels and mediums of education, e.g. OpenCourseWare exchange, exchanges between the water and education sectors, facilitating the transfer of ideas from research into education and training, or possible policies that allow curricula and materials to be co-developed and shared by groups of university/school lecturers.

The workshop will be based on experiences from many fields of education around the world, especially from:

- School education;
- Vocational education and training;
- Higher education; and
- Community and stakeholder education (including the media).

Expected outcome

Focusing on best practices and teaching approaches from around the world will allow discussing and defining global and regionally adapted education approaches to water issues, use and management in K-12/school education, vocational education and training, higher education, and community and stake-holder education. Discussions around the four conference objectives specified above will take place to overview current status. Recommendations for action on global, regional and national level will be reinforced as input into the closing plenary and the Bonn Declaration, to be adopted in the closing plenary session. These recommendations, that will follow-up on the recommendations of previous international conferences and of the UNESCO Regional Workshops on Water Education. The recommendations of these Regional Workshops will be further strengthened after the UNESCO World ESD Conference via consultations with Member States via UNESCO National Commissions (particularly IHP National Committees), with the UNESCO Intersectoral Platform on Education for Sustainable Development, with UN Agencies (via UN-Water) and other intergovernmental bodies.

The water and education related workshop will also strengthen the linkages between the United Nations Decade of Education for Sustainable Development and the International Decade for Action 'Water for Life', by developing a consolidated approach to strengthen training and education.

Support materials

Background support materials and inputs include:

For all levels of education:

- Outcomes of the UNESCO Regional Water and Ed-ucation Workshops (UNESCO IHP, in partnership with UNESCO-IHE, UNW-DPC, UNESCO-UNEVOC, ASPNet, UNITWIN, Itaipu Binacional and other partners)

School education:

- Great Volga River Route (UNESCO ASPNet)
- WASH in Schools (UNICEF/IRC): http://www. schools.watsan.net
- Living on the Edge (UNEP/GEMS): http://unep.org/tunza/youth/Publications/wesc_brochure%5B1% 5D.pdf
- World Water Monitoring Day (WEF/IWA): http://www.worldwatermonitoringday.org

- Water Education for Teachers (WET): http://www.projectwet.org, including its activities in developing countries (e.g. UNESCO IHP LAC/Project WET Water and Education Programme)
- The Blue Planet initiative (UNESCO/Weizmann Institute)
- Voices of Youth (UNICEF): http://www.unicef.org/voy/explore/wes/explore_1818.html
- Water in DESD in Sweden: Side Event 2008 Stockholm World Water Week 'What Did You Learn in School Today?' http://www.worldwaterweek. org/programme/monday/mon05-whatlearnschool-today.asp
- Water in DESD in Germany: Annual Theme 2008 'Water' (GUK): http://www.bne-portal.de/wasser
- Water in DESD in Germany: Symposium 'Water—Education—Future': http://www.bne-portal.de/wassertagung

Vocational education and training:

- TVET(UNESCO-UNEVOC): http://www.unevoc.unesco.org
- VET(BIBB/BMU): http://www.bibb.de

Higher education:

- Sets of materials developed by UNESCO-IHE Insti-tute for Higher Education (www.unesco-ihe.org), the water-related centres operating under the auspices of UNESCO, and the water related UNESCO Chairs.
- E-learning/Blended Learning (German UNESCO-IHP/WMO-HWRP National Committee): http://www.lfi.rwth-aachen.de and http://totwat.lfi.rwth-aachen.de

- Bi-cultural MSc Courses:
  - — IWRM (BMZ, DAAD, Cologne University of Applied Sciences/Amman University): http://www.iwrm-master.info
  - — Environment and Resources Management (DAAD, Cologne University of Applied Sciences/ Universidad Autonoma de San Luis Potosi): http://www.tt.fh-koeln.de/forms/Application%20form_ENREM%20Master_2008. doc
- NeWater OpenCourseWare Curriculum on Adaptive River Basin Management: http://wiki.gwsp.org/moodle

Community and stakeholder education:

- Integrated Water Resources Management TOOL-BOX (Global Water Partnership)
- We All Use Water (Australian Water Association)
- US EPA Education Resources
- Sustainable Wastewater Management for smaller communities (New Zealand)

CHAPTER

Workshop—2

Strengthening the Educational Response to Climate Change Internationally?

Rationale

Science has now shown that:

- human activities are perturbing the whole Earth-system at a wide-scale and with extreme speed, affecting the cycles of all major components of life: water, carbon, nitrogen etc. In particular, the massive CO_2 emissions from burning fossil-fuel and deforestation is driving global warming (and thus increases in sea level), ocean acidification, and a wealth of inter-dependent effects that we are unable to predict with reasonable certainty.
- the risks involved for humanity range from massive loss of biodiversity, huge costs to the economy, and tragedy for billions of people unable to adapt due to poverty, loss of land, scarcity of drinking water and other related afflictions.
- the only way to stop taking such dangerous risks is to decrease and progressively stop emitting greenhouse gases (GHG) into the atmosphere.

The dominant development model in the world, based on continued industrialisation and economic growth, is characterised by massive use of fossil fuel, intensive agriculture and deforestation—which coupled with demographic growth lead to large increases in GHG emissions. It is therefore completely impossible to stop or drastically reduce our emissions from one day to the next. So the key question for society is: how to change this unsustainable civilization into a sustainable one without jeopardizing it, and at what pace? How can we progressively stop using fossil fuels, stop deforestation, stabilize population growth, and at the same time, ensure that basic living conditions are satisfied for all?

The changes required are not just minor adjustments to mainstream pathways nor reverting to a 'stone-age society', but rather a change of paradigm and culture *toward global citizenship.* A complete re-thinking of our production and consumption patterns, and lifestyles. A new society which addresses the issues of global justice and global commons (such as our shared atmosphere and water) which go well beyond the traditional boundaries of national interest and current environmental policies. The challenge is clear:

1. Ultimately, a sustainable world means a zero-emissions world, where use of non-renewable natural resources (e.g. coal and oil) has been replaced by use of renewable resources and all waste is recycled.
2. Several countries, including the EU, currently promote in international climate negotiations the goal of staying 'below the 2-degree limit'—a level proposed as the threshold under which we could avoid 'dangerous climate change'. Model projections indicate that this level can be obtained only by a reduction of the world's greenhouse gas emissions to half of their 1990 levels by 2050. To achieve this, with a world population potentially reaching 9 billion by 2050, we will need to reduce emissions to about 2 tons of CO_2-equivalent per capita, which means *cutting them by a factor of 5 to 10 in the developed world.*

3. In 2008, 20 years after the creation of the IPCC and 16 years after the United Nations gave a mandate to 'achieve stabilisation of GHG concentrations', humanity has not yet started to reduce its emissions. Instead, emissions are still growing exponentially. This discouraging situation is primarily due to strong growth in the developing world (particularly in nations experiencing rapid industrialisation, like China) and because industrialised countries, despite their previous commitments and initial efforts, are still continuing to increase their emissions (notably in the transport sector).
4. In 2007, the IPCC predicted that: in *Africa* by 2020, between 75 million and 250 million people are projected to be exposed to increased water stress. Agricultural production in many countries, including access to food, is projected to be severely compromised by climate variability and change. In *Asia* by 2050, decreasing freshwater availability in most areas could put more than a billion people at risk. Increased deaths and illness are expected from cholera and from diarrhoea! diseases, associated with increased flooding and drought that result from higher sea temperatures. In *Small Island Developing States,* rising sea levels and increased storm surges will threaten the homes and livelihoods of communities, and will force displacement and permanent migration.

The emission trends will most likely not go down before international agreements lead to ambitious policies combining incentives (taxes) and constraints (laws) on a global scale. But while governments are struggling with negotiations and policy, individuals can act immediately, and schools and community groups are undoubtedly onc of the most critical link to families and young people. *It is the empowerment of the individuals that will drive the necessary behavioural change and enable higher level institutions to move forward with policies, strategies and incentives for industry and society to transform.*

Climate change education—from transmissive to transformative

The world's population is young, with some 2.2 billion people under the age of 18. All over the world, these children and young people, representing nearly one-third of the global population, are concerned with the increasing threat posed by rising global carbon emissions and the changing climate. Many are already experiencing the impacts of the changing global environment in their communities. Despite all of this, to date children and young people have been relatively absent in climate change policies and plans which are being developed by many countries and regions in response to existing and emerging international agreements and protocols which support these initiatives.

Based on the premise that what children learn today will shape the world tomorrow, instilling environmental awareness at a young age is the best way, ultimately, to protect the environment. Adaptation and mitigation programmes that improve the availability and quality of environmental education are key interventions for long-term change. However, increasing environmental awareness is not enough. For children and youth to become effective agents of change, avenues must exist for their knowledge to be translated into advocacy and action.

In that respect climate change education needs to be transformative—in the sense developed in the UNESCO's Policy Dialogue paper 'ESD and CC'—and for this needs to integrate three pillars:

1. *Contents and knowledge*: Understanding the facts, the scale of the challenge, the potential consequences, the solutions available and the governance strategies that can lead towards sustainable development pathways. This relates in particular to interdisciplinary science education, where a key challenge is to make science

learning more exciting, more concrete, more experimental, more connected to real-life problems.

2. *Values and representations*: Forging global citizenship and the feeling of belonging to one same planet and one same humanity. Understanding that it is not only nature and the planet which are in danger, but the life conditions for a peaceful cohabitation of billions of humans;
3. *Behaviour change and citizenship competences*: Developing the capacity to take action for changing the course in society, both locally and globally.

The last two pillars are particularly challenging for schools who are traditionally (with variations depending on countries) less prepared to work on values, behaviours and competences than on transmitting knowledge and facts. However, such values and behaviours are often developed and encouraged in community and youth group settings. The workshop should identify strategies for strengthening the capacity of school systems in these domains and the possible links with non-formal education mechanisms.

Ultimately, the key question for climate change education is the same one as for ESD at large: *in a society still broadly dominated by a non-sustainable culture, how can schools contribute to promoting safe, healthy and sustainable lifestyles?*

The workshop shall bring new creative and daring ideas for changing the scale of action for ESD in daily classroom practice, from marginal to mainstream, from sectorised to integrated, towards a deep transformation of education systems to train future citizen equipped with the understanding, values and skills to achieve sustainability. In that respect the outcomes of workshop will constitute a direct input to the Kyoto-2 negotiation roadmap, in full line with the statement expressed by the Education Caucus of the United Nations Commission on Sustainable Development (CSD) at the recent COP14 meeting in Poznan:

"INVESTING IN A WELL-PREPARED SOCIETY: ENVIRONMENTAL EDUCATION, IS THE CRUCIAL BUILDING BLOCK IN KYOTO 2

It is clear in the Bali roadmap that much attention has been given to the four building blocks:

— *adaptation, mitigation, finance, technology*

— *as the basis of the policy framework for the second set of Kyoto commitments. However, given the complexities of the current global challenges, mitigating climate change can exacerbate or worsen biodiversity loss, water shortages, food security, and poverty reduction. As we look to Copenhagen, the fifth building block is missing. It is time to ask, What are Stakeholders, Governments and Civil Society Organisations doing about Environmental Education and Sustainability?"*

CHAPTER

Workshop—3

Advancing Sustainable Lifestyles and Responsible Consumption through ESD

Consumption has become the socio-economic driving force and the core value of an increasing number of societies worldwide. In both developing and developed countries, unsustainable patterns of consumption also have serious impacts on people and the environment. For this reason, and given its cross-cutting dimension, responsible consumption, otherwise called sustainable consumption, is certainly at the core of Education for Sustainable Development (ESD). Education for Sustainable Consumption (ESC) plays a key role in the main social and environmental challenges addressed in this conference. Through the parameters of equity and sustainability, ESC contributes to turn consumption into a bearer of well-being, peace and human development.

Objectives of the Workshop

This workshop will focus on Education for Sustainable Consumption (ESC) in formal, non-formal and informal education as an integral part of ESD, building on the values

Here and Now! Education for Sustainabie Consumption. Recommendations and Guidelines

Here and Now! is aimed at policy makers, educational institutions and actors, and mostly focuses on formal education. The document contains three sections (I-Addressing the challenges; II-Cptimizing opportunities; III-Relevant resources), and stands *as* an instrument for policy-making and integration of ESC into education and sustainable development strategies.

Here and Now! is also aimed at providing educators and trainers with pedagogical information and tools. The guidelines have been developed in order to help fulfill the recommendations of the Johannesburg Plan of Implementation with regards the elaboration of a 10-year Framework of Programmes for Sustainabie Consumption and Production (Marrakech Process).

Here and Now! have notably been drafted in close collaboration with the Consumer Citizenship Network (CCN), an interdisciplinary network of educators, researchers and civil society organizations representing 136 institutions in 37 countries that was created in 2003 to work on education for sustainable consumption and global solidarity (for further information: http:// www.hihm.no/concit/).

Here and Now! can be downloaded at http:// www.unep.fr/scp/marrakech/taskforces/education.htm and will be available in the virtual library of the Conference.

upon which ESD is founded: the training of responsible citizens and consumers, aware of their fundamental rights and freedoms, informed to participate in the public debate and oriented towards a critical participation in the market. This definition needs to be deepened and strengthened by a clear understanding of each context to which it applies, as well as of its North-South dimension. Finally, the workshop will also aim at highlighting the value of education and responsible consumption in the context of the economic and financial crisis the whole world is currently facing.

Through creative and interactive discussions, the workshop will provide participants with the opportunity to share experiences, gain insights and consult on ways forward for the next five years of the UN Decade on ESD on how to formulate, stimulate, carry out and evaluate education for sustainable consumption. In this framework, it will consider how the recent guidelines presented in *Here and Now! Education for Sustainable Consumption,* jointly developed by the United Nations Environment Programme, the Marrakech Task Force on ESC led by Italy[1] and the Hedmark University College, stands as a tool to assist policymakers, teachers and parents in implementation ESC.

Responsible Consumption for Sustainable Societies

Why advancing sustainable lifestyles and responsible consumption should be considered as one of the core objectives of BSD? The project of developing sustainable lifestyles aims at providing individuals with the means to build their identity and socialize through practices and choices enabling them to meet their needs and aspirations with a sense of responsibility. Not only as economic actors but also as citizens, individuals are encouraged to take into account the social and environmental impacts of these practices and choices. This requires the setting of a new ground work to rethink the way everyday life is organized as well as our visions for the future. Responsible consumption patterns stands for a crucial component of this process. On the one

---

[1] The Marrakech Process on Sustainable Consumption and Production (SCP) is a global multistakeholder process to promote SCP and to elaborate a 10-year Framework of Programmes to support regional and national implementation of SCP. The Marrakech Task Force on Education for Sustainable Consumption was launched during the 14th Session of the United Nations Commission on Sustainable Development (CSD14—New York, May 2006) as a tangible contribution of Italy to the Marrakech Process. For more information: http://www.unep.fr/scp/marrakech/taskforces/education.htm

hand, responsible consumption deals with all aspects of everyday life and in this sense needs to be approached as a crosscutting issue encapsulating lifestyles as a whole (attitudes, relation to nature and to the others, responsibility towards one's community, behaviors as an economic actor, etc.). On the other hand, the development of more responsible patterns of consumption, notably based on a better understanding of life-cycles, will positively impact on the environment, societies and communities, the achievement of the UN Millennium Goals and the advancement of human rights.

Education for Sustainable Consumption: a definition

In the framework of ESD, ESC has the potential to become a new educational paradigm aimed at raising education levels without creating an ever-growing demand for resources and consumer goods, and at fostering responsible individual and collective choices towards the environment and society. From formal education to awareness-raising, the ambition of ESC is to empower people so that they are able to responsibly manage their social and environmental impacts, but also to participate in and stimulate the public debate about values, quality of life, responsibility and accountability. ESC finally consists of nothing less than the acquisition of knowledge, attitudes and skills necessary for functioning in today's society, with three complementary objectives at a collective level: a rational utilization of natural resources necessary to human life, an equitable economic and social development, a better quality of life for all.

This is the reason why it has been widely recognized that, provided its holistic dimension, ESC should be designed as a transversal approach requiring multi-stakeholder cooperation, more specifically at the local level, and the involvement of all actors: public authorities, educational institutions and actors, youth networks, civil society, businesses, development and cooperation actors. One of the objectives is the promotion of cultural diversity and traditional knowledge. Indeed, local environments and cultures need to be taken into account to integrate the culture of sustainable consumption into people's habits and attitudes, based on a sense of citizenship towards their environment and community.

Agenda for discussions

This background information sets the context for specific themes to be discussed by the participants, together with resource persons who are expected to actively and significantly contribute to the debate by bringing their expertise to the workshop. Resource persons will animate the discussions and assist in drawing the conclusions of the workshop on each discussion themes.

(a) Engaging policy-makers and providing resources for ESC

One of the conditions required to develop and mainstream ESC in all education fields—from formal education to public communication—is to raise awareness of public and private decision-makers towards responsible investments in sustainable consumption and production patterns. Involving relevant ministries, in particular economics and finance, in providing financial support to ESC practices and research in the framework of ESD also stands as a priority. In this perspective, the workshop will discuss and highlight the opportunities offered by ESC with regards to national and regional strategies for sustainable development.

(b) Integrating ESC into formal education

From primary schools to universities, formal education is one of the main drivers of development and plays a key role in advancing sustainable lifestyles and consumption. In this framework, ESC first needs to be given coherence and consistency as an inter-disciplinary topic in *programmes and curricula.* Despite increased awareness of the human impact on the environment and a greater focus on the consequences of individual lifestyle choices, sustainable consumption is still not always seen as a central topic in educational systems and policies. For ESC to be successfully integrated into educational curricula, teachers and trainers also need to understand its relevance in education patterns as well as in their own disciplines. This notably implies a reorientation of *teacher training*, allowing access to educational resources and building networks on teaching/learning processes. Furthermore, ESC relies on the ongoing and coherent development of *pedagogical approaches and tools*, notably to enable a common understanding of ESC among teaching and pedagogical staff, facilitate interdisciplinary cooperation and mainstream ESC in established subjects. The fact that didactic resources are numerous but also fragmented and difficult to use in an interdisciplinary perspective stands as an issue in this regards. *Educational institutions and schools* also need to be encouraged to integrate sustainable consumption into their management systems (sustainable procurement, equipment, building management, public administration and services, participation of staff and students in school events on sustainable consumption, etc). As part of the objectives of School Agenda 21, this fully contributes to the promotion of sustainable consumption as a concrete and legitimate issue among teachers and students.

(c) ESC as *a life-long process: talking to citizens, changing behaviours*

ESC is a life-long process and is not restricted to formal or non-formal education aimed at children and young people. For society to evolve towards sustainable consumption and production patterns, communication and public information, *awareness-raising* initietives are necessary. Those actions participate in building new values and in motivating the adoption of new behaviours. Communication campaigns on sustainable consumption, at the international, national and local levels, led by public institutions as well as by NGOs and businesses, have been multiplying to inform, sensitize, influence citizens' perceptions and behaviors and support public policies. However, the gap between people's recognition of and commitment to sustainability issues and their actual consumption habits remains a real challenge in terms of communication, primarily for public institutions but also for non-governmental actors involved in the sensitization of citizens.

(d) Measurement and evaluation

Efficient ESC implementation rests on a good understanding of contexts and populations. In this regards, research and reporting have a core role to play. Evaluating ESC also means assessing the impacts of policies and actions. Therefore, every project, from formal to non-formal education and life-long learning, should include clear targets and evaluation objectives that can be used for future developments and shared among ESC actors. Indicators of different kinds can be used: such as a number of partners involved in the project, population reached, impact in the media, life-length of the project, economic benefits including social and environmental criteria, impacts on representations and behaviours (through surveys, market research with the contribution of businesses, etc.). But most importantly, sharing tools and good practices as well as developing quality indicators stand as key perspectives for ESC assessment.

For each of the workshop themes, the discussions will focus on three simple questions:

(i) What are the lessons learnt?
(ii) What is the vision?
(iii) How can we achieve it?

The multi-stakeholder dimension of ESC should be considered as a transversal issue and highlighted throughout the discussions. In addition, more specific questions will be provided to the participants in the workshop in preparation of the Conference.

CHAPTER

Workshop—4

ESD and Disaster Risk Reduction *Building Disaster-Resilient Societies*

Learning to live with risk

Education for sustainable development and disaster risk reduction :

"More effective prevention strategies would save not only tens of billions of dollars, but save tens of thousands of lives. Funds currently spent on intervention and relief could be devoted to enhancing equitable and sustainable development instead, which would further reduce the risk for war and disaster. Building a culture of prevention is not easy. While the costs of prevention have to be paid in the present, its benefits lie in a distant future. Moreover, the benefits are not tangible; they are the disasters that did NOT happen."

Kofi Annan

Former UN Secretary-General: "Introduction to Secretary-General's Annual Report on the Work of the Organization of United Nations, 1999" (document A/54/1)

Introduction on Disaster Risk Reduction and Education for Sustainable Development

The occurrences of natural disasters are on the rise. Images of the devastating Myanmar cyclone and China Sichuan earthquake are painful reminders of the world's increasing vulnerability. In 2008, 321 disasters killed 235 816 people, affected 211 million others and cost a total of US$ 181 billion. Asia was the most affected continent. The death toll in 2008 was three times more than the annual average of 66812 for 2000-2007.

Hazards are part of nature but can turn into disasters as a result of human interactions. The continued failure to manage natural resources, the demographic pressure and human settlements in fragile ecosystems and the increased demand on environment, are among the main causes of environmental degradation and comes in addition to the threat of global climate change and rising sea levels. The IPCC studies predict that climate change—contributed to by human activities—will increase and intensify the extension of natural events and exacerbate the underlying risk many developing countries are already facing.

Disasters are among the biggest obstacles to achieving the UN's Millennium Development Goals for poverty reduction. Thus, reducing disaster risks and their impact has become an important development issue in its own right. Since the United Nations Conference on Environment and Development (UNCED) in Rio de Janeiro, in 1992, disaster reduction has been recognized as an integral component of sustainable development (Chapter 3 of Agenda 21). This conclusion and the cross-cutting nature of disaster risk reduction were once again underlined in 2002 at the World Summit on Sustainable Development.

The international implementation scheme of the Decade of Education for Sustainable Development (2005-2014) in fact sees disaster preparedness and mitigation are critical issues.

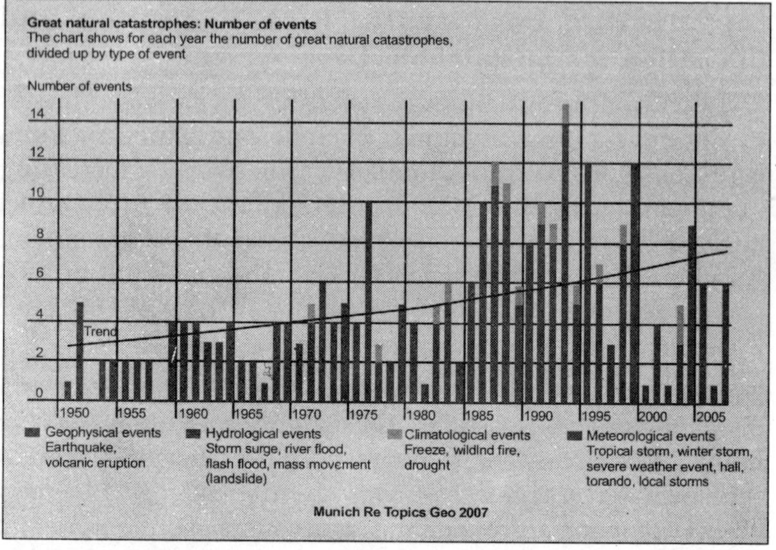

In this regard, Mr. Ko'i'chiro Matsuura, Director-General of UNESCO, highlighted the significant role of education in improving the capacity of individuals and communities to reduce the risk of disasters: "anticipating, educating and informing are the keys to reducing the deadly effects of such natural disasters" (3 January, 2005).

This goal is supported by the Hyogo Framework for Action 2005-2015: "Building the Resilience of Nations and Communities to Disasters", as adopted at the World Conference on Disaster Reduction, 2005, Kobe, Japan, which highlights the importance of education and learning as part of its priorities for action, using knowledge, innovation and education to build a culture of safety and resilience at all levels.

Therefore Education for Disaster Risk Reduction (EDRR) as part of Disaster Risk Reduction (DRR) has to be inherent with Education for Sustainable Development (ESD) and supports the frameworks of ESD in three important ways:

- Education for Disaster Risk Reduction is interdisciplinary. Therefore, important consideration is given to the impacts on, and relationship between, society, the environment, economy and culture.

- Education for Disaster Risk Reduction promotes critical thinking and problem solving and other social and emotional life skills that are essential to the empowerment of stakeholder groups threatened or affected by disasters.
- Education for Disaster Risk Reduction supports the Millennium Development Goals. Without considering Disaster Risk Reduction in development planning, all efforts including, decades of development initiatives could be destroyed in seconds.

The conference workshop 'ESD and disaster risk reduction: building disaster-resilient societies'

The goal of this workshop is to re-examine the notion of education for disaster risk reduction and its contributing role in the Decade by successfully confronting disaster risk as a key sustainable development challenge. In correspondence with one of the major thrusts of ESD to reorient curricula towards sustainable development, as identified in Chapter 36 of Agenda 21, the participants of the workshop will review achievements made so far in disaster risk education and identify mechanisms and activities to further promote and strengthen education for disaster risk reduction in formal and non-formal settings in the second half of the Decade. The workshop will build around the following five strategic themes, to be introduced through best practices and challenges at international, national, regional, and local level.

Strategic Theme 1: 'Advocacy to Policy Makers'

The incorporation of disaster risk reduction in education for sustainable development is a legitimate matter of public policy at the highest national levels for three main reasons. The first one is public safety and the protection of human life. The second is the protection of the nation's resource base and productive assets (infrastructure and private property or investments) to ensure long-term development and economic growth. The third is that States, as duty-bearers, shall undertake appropriate policy, legislative and administrative measures to facilitate the implementation of the children's rights recognized in the International bill of human Rights and in the Convention on the Rights of the Child.

Strategic Theme 2: 'Capacity Building'

Capacity building is the process and means through which national governments and local communities develop the necessary skills and expertise to manage their environment and natural resources in a sustainable manner. Institutions and communities, which execute policy decisions, must be educated and trained on how to locally optimize disaster reduction measures in order to handle such risks.

Strategic Theme 3: 'Formal Education'

To create a culture of safety, disaster risk reduction and environmental issues, have to be integrated within all levels of education, from the pre-primary to the advanced university levels. The following three complementary elements are important for long-term sustainability in mainstreaming disaster risk reduction in formal education: (1) Curricula and school integration; (2) Teacher training; (3) Assessment of learning. These three elements furthermore need to be aligned to ensure coherency. One of the major challenges relies in making the complex cause-effect chains between human behaviour and environment comprehendible to children and youth, and to ensure that they are and will, as future citizens be able to make sound decisions and act upon these in their lives through increased life-skills and knowledge.

Strategic Theme 4: 'Non-formal Education'

Non-formal education can be the rapid entry point for disaster risk reduction education. This can take many forms, offering fun and engaging ways to introduce important knowledge, skills and competencies for students of all ages. Within recent years more interest has been generated in the understanding of indigenous and traditional knowledge and the realisation of its potential to improve disaster risk reduction policies, especially through the linkage with disaster education and early warning systems.

Strategic Theme 5: 'Educational Infrastructure'

A safe education facility is that which is either located in a danger-free zone or has been built to be resilient to an extreme natural event. Educational infrastructure can be made resilient through measures such as land use planning, structural reinforcement and emergency plans. Older school buildings should also be made resilient and to that end, should benefit from effective retrofitting programmes.

Guiding questions and workshop methodology

The workshop intends to address the following guiding questions:

- Why is it imperative to incorporate Disaster Risk Reduction into Education for Sustainable Development?
- Which are the key issues that need to be considered when incorporating Disaster Risk Reduction into Education for Sustainable Development?
- How can we create synergetic effects between the Disaster Risk Reduction and Education for Sustainable Development community?
- Which elements of Disaster Risk Reduction seem universal and transferable from industrialized countries to developing countries, or by south-south exchange?
- Where can I find additional information on this topic?

Recommendations and action items for the next five years of the decade are developed and discussed in a participatory manner with the audience and resource experts from the field of Education for Disaster Risk Reduction. A policy document linking education for disaster risk reduction and education for sustainable development will be shared and discussed with the participants.

In the workshop a variety of formats are used like presentations, group discussions, panels, expert consultations, and other dialog formats that allows the entire group to participate in the discussion, including collaboration with other conference workshops being intended.

Workshop—5

Educating for Food Security *Contribution of ESD*

The objective of the workshop is to highlight that Education is an essential prerequisite for reducing poverty, improving agriculture and living condition of rural people and building a sustainable and food secure world and to address the challenges and good practices and example to promote education and food security.

Another 40 million people have been pushed into hunger this year primarily due to higher food prices, according to preliminary estimates published by FAO today. This brings the overall number of undernourished people in the world to 963 million, compared to 923 million in 2007 and the ongoing financial and economic crisis could tip even more people into hunger and poverty. The structural problems of hunger, like the lack of access to land, credit and employment, combined with high food prices remain a dire reality. The 1996 World Food Summit target, to reduce the number of hungry by half by 2015, requires a strong political commitment and investment in poor countries of at least $30 billion per year for agriculture and social protection of the poor. The vast majority of the world's undernourished people—907 million—live in developing countries, according to the 2007 data reported by the State of Food Insecurity in the World. The world hunger situation may further deteriorate as the financial crisis hits the real economies of more and more countries (FAO 9/9/2008). It is therefore urgent to address the education needs of the poor and food insecure, most of whom live and work in rural areas, where increased production needs to take place and foster rural people's capacities and resilience to deal with today's challenges.

The workshop is part of the international actions aiming at contributing to eradicating extreme poverty and hunger and promoting sustainable development by increasing access to quality education.

It focuses especially on the impact of education on food security.

The vision that inspires this workshop is that people—not institutions or technology—are the driving force of development, as the United Nations Millennium Declaration indicates. Research on the role and impact of education in development has led to the conclusion that universal basic education, and specifically Education for Rural People, is (Burchi De Muro 2007) the neglected key to food security. A recent study conducted by FAO and The University of Rome 3 found that the correlation between food security and primary education is very high although it decreases at other educational levels. More over, research addressing the link between education and agriculture income and productivity has a long tradition.

The workshop will address Universal Primary Education and Education for Rural People as key efforts to achieve the Millenium Development Goals (MDGs). Rural people, who are the majority of the world poor, need to be included in the education systems and in socio-economic development. The workshop will address the main challenges, lessons and good prac-tices to promote ERP at all levels of the education system. ERP is as crucial to building open, democratic and modern societies, contrary to societies reproducing urban elites that control economic and social power and foster exclusion and segregation of rural people and producers. In a knowledge-based society segregation and exclusion of rural people from education is directly related to their exclusion from food and wealth, knowledge and work, health, citizenship, political participation and representation, thus undermining a democratic society and fostering social strife and violence. The workshop will focus on the crucial role of ERP and School Feeding in developing the capacities needed to address the challenges of globalization and specifically the crisis of high food prices and of climate change.

Higher food prices impound further the progress made so far. As a matter of fact, on current trends, the 2015 goal of Universal Primary Education will be missed: in 2006 some 75 million children of primary school age were not in school. This is 12 per cent of the developing world's primary-school-age population. In sub-Saharan Africa, nearly one-third of that age group is out of school. Girls still account for the majority of the world's out-of-school children (55%). Using a partial projection covering countries that account for just two-thirds of the 75 million primary school age children out of school today, 29 million children will still be out of school in 2015.

Since the majority of the 75 million out-of-school children come from rural areas of poor, food deficit countries, these are affected disproportionately by the crisis in their attainment of the Education For All Goals. Vulnerable households with low purchasing power resort to negative coping strategies, which include sale of scarce assets, extensive borrowing which lead to getting heavily into debt, reducing quantity and quality of daily meals, and compromising nutritional status by consuming less nutritious foods. Poor households are obliged to choose between sending their children to school or to the fields, to work for food. The family meal of today takes priority over the children's potential for tomorrow. The price crunch means that, across the developing world, poor families which may have had money to pay school fees for their children, to go to clinics when they are sick, or take much-needed nourishing food together with anti-retroviral drugs, will suffer as they cut back in these areas. They are cutting meals and substituting less nutritious foods.

While it may be too early to estimate with certainty the fallout from the unprecedented high food prices crisis on Education For All Goals, the consequences are certain. Global inequalities in education mirror inequalities in income. The association is not coincidental. While the relationship between education and wealth creation is complex, knowledge is an important driver for sustainable development and food security. In the short run, protecting the most vulnerable require direct food distribution, targeted food subsidies and cash transfers, and nutritional programmes including school feeding. The precise choice will depend on the extent to which some form of safety net or social protection mechanisms are already in place and can be mobilized.

Well organized and targeted social protection systems are potentially capable of providing direct support to the neediest at a cost that is substantially lower than more broad-based actions which, in turn, makes them more sustainable. Systems such as WFP's VAM—Vulnerability Analysis and Mapping can support UN Agencies, Governments and NGOs in making informed targeting choices of a wide range of food security, poverty reduction and education programmes. Wide and in-depth analysis, supported by the latest geospatial and mapping systems helps prioritize scarce overseas development assistance re-sources to where they are most needed.

New partnerships are also needed to raise farmer productivity and income through improved farming systems, supply of farm inputs, training of farmers and increased availability of markets. Innovative initiatives such as the NEPAD 'Home Grown School Feeding' which aims at providing school children (adequately targeted) with locally produced food are taking should be expanded. The Home Grown School Feeding approach is holistic and integrated as it aims—on the one side—to: *(i)* provide incentives for education (both enrolment and retention of girls and boys) and responses to nutritional gaps and 'short term' hunger and on the other side; *(ii)* create opportunities for stimulating and improving local farmers' production, expanding local demand and increase local market value.

Working with national governments and alongside bilateral partners, United Nations agencies, NGOs, farmers, traders, processors and research institutions, initiatives such as WFP's the 'Purchase For Progress' will help create a platform of demand for food staples grown by small farmers. The aim is to help reduce the risks farmers face and boost incentives to invest in technologies and practices to increase and improve production.

The Purchase for Progress ('P4P') initiative aims to:

- identify and share best practices for WFP, NGOs, governments and agricultural market stakeholders to increase profitable engagement in markets;
- increase farmers' capacities in order to raise their income from agricultural markets;
- identify and implement best practices for increasing sales by low-income farmers to WFP.

The following table (*See on next page*) serves as a general outline to guide the working group discussion:

The regulatory role of the state will also be addressed in ensuring equitable access to education as a key public good. 'School Reform' through devolution from the centre to periphery, from state to private, to communities and to civil society through cost-sharing will be discussed given that

Challenges, Lessons and Examples in Education for Rural People

Challenges	Lessons	Examples
Effective pro-rural policies	Urban and rural EMIS disaggregated data. Policies recognize the diversity of needs of rural people, their agro-ecological and geographical circumstances and their socio-economic and cultural characteristics.	A strategy for Education for Rural People in Kosovo: 2004-2009 prepared by the Ministry of Education and the Ministry of Agriculture
Organizational Efficiency	Government ownership of education programmes. Co-ordination among ministries of education and agriculture, extension, schools, NGOs and the private sector is essential for optimal efficiency.	Rural teachers, trained in technical subjects ensure curriculum relevance and support extension programmes. Extension officers provide presentations in schools, conduct adult education classes, and organize farmer field schools.
Flexibility and local autonomy	Systems can combine national and local curriculum planning through community participation. Flexibility in the academic calendar to accommodate weather, cropping patterns nomadic movements.	In Thailand, 40% of the curriculum can be based on community and local needs. In Mozambique 20% of the curriculum is decentralized.

(Contd...)

Challenges	Lessons	Examples
Access and quality	School Feeding programmes to improve access to universal primary education. School attendance benefits from fee removal or reduction; free access to learning materials; and new school construction. Some countries promote teacher training, for context specific learning and develop training materials designed to address real rural life problems and for life skills. Quality of education, provision of a safe and adequate learning environment.	Double-shift classes and after-hours adult education; targeting of specific rural groups; satellite schools for the youngest children in remote areas; application of ICT and farmer participation in curriculum planning and managing education and training events.
Parent and community involvement	Participatory, community-based approaches help to in-crease educational access and quality and community ownership of schools Rural families want to see that the education of their children is relevant to rural livelihoods.	Parent-teacher bodies have impact on school resources; improved monitoring of quality and relevance and for school lunch programmes.
Skills training for rural people	Formal and non-formal life skills training for adults and school drop-outs help rural people diversify their skills and provide literacy and numeracy for more secure livelihoods and greater resilience during times of stress and disaster.	Junior Farmer Field and Life Schools in Mozambique that deal with agricultural as well as life skills development among young rural citizens.

(Contd...)

Challenges	Lessons	Examples
Redefining agricultural education	EARTH University in Costa Rica has four pillars to its pro-grammes: Social Commitment; Environmental Awareness; Entrepreneurial Mentality; and Development of Human Values	Agricultural education that reflects changes in technology; global supply chains; health challenges; on and off farm employment; environmental changes and enterprise development.
Recruitment and retention of teachers and extension staff	Attract teachers and extension workers from rural areas. Develop attractive deployment policies including: bonuses and higher salaries, provision of subsidized housing, posting newly qualified staff in pairs and creating career progression options	Malaysia: incentives that include a piece of land and training in agriculture to encourage teachers to stay in rural areas. Lao PDR: profit sharing in school-based income-generating activities for students and teachers.
Gender responsive environments	Flexible timetables to accommodate peak labour demand for girls and adult women.Well-supervised boarding facilities safeguard female children. School meals for all children Take-home rations for girls an incentive for families to send girls to school.	Half-day long farmer training short courses geared toward women that have responsibilities at home.

privatization might increase exclusion and inequality and abdicate the role of the state to provide quality life-long education to all. Transformation of education (including extension) from a public good into merchandise is more and more pervasive and is a challenge that jeopardizes rural people inclusion in the global community and wealth and their contribution to sustainable development therefore, increasing the risk of global food crises.

CHAPTER

Workshop—6

AIDS, Health and Education for Sustainable Development

Health and Sustainable Development

Health is at the center of human aspirations and a basic right, resource and outcome for sustainable development. Health cuts across all Millennium Development Goals (MDGs), while 3 of the 8 MDGs focus on health: reducing child mortality; improving maternal health; and combating HIV/AIDS, malaria and other diseases. The goals of sustainable development cannot be achieved when there is a high prevalence of debilitating illnesses.

The Bonn Call for Action on Promoting Sustainable Global Health 2007 emphasizes that:

- *Good health is good wealth*—Health is the bed-rock of economic prosperity, and fosters improved human productivity and, consequently, better investment opportunities;
- *Good health is good governance*—A healthy work-force, safe living and working conditions, social health

protection, and access to water and sanitation foster stable cities, rural areas, and societies; and

- **Good health is good for security and peace building**—Providing sufficient health services to all is not only an expression of social solidarity, but the foundation of social stability and sustainable development, and an indispensable pillar of human security.

Despite steady gains in past decades towards the fulfillment of the MDGs, the health-related MDGs remain those least likely to be achieved by 2015, based on current rates of progress.

Health and Education

The goal of universal education cannot be achieved while the health needs of children and adolescents remain unmet. The expanded commentary on the Dakar Framework for Action describes three ways in which health relates to the achievement of Education for All (EFA):

- *as* an *input and condition necessary for learning;*
- *as* an *outcome of effective quality education;* and
- *as a sector that must collaborate with education* to achieve the goal of EFA.

HIV & AIDS and Education in a Spiral

The impact of ill health on the education sector can be exemplified by HIV and AIDS. In highly-affected countries, the AIDS epidemic is eroding the capacity of the education sector, causing shortages of teachers and education staff, increasing the vulnerability of children and learners, and adding new difficulties for planning.

On the other hand, world leaders have agreed that education is a powerful tool for meeting goals aimed at improved health. The education sector has an es-sential advocacy role to play in highlighting the links between health and its determinants, and empowering individuals with values, knowledge and skills to maintain health-seeking behaviours.

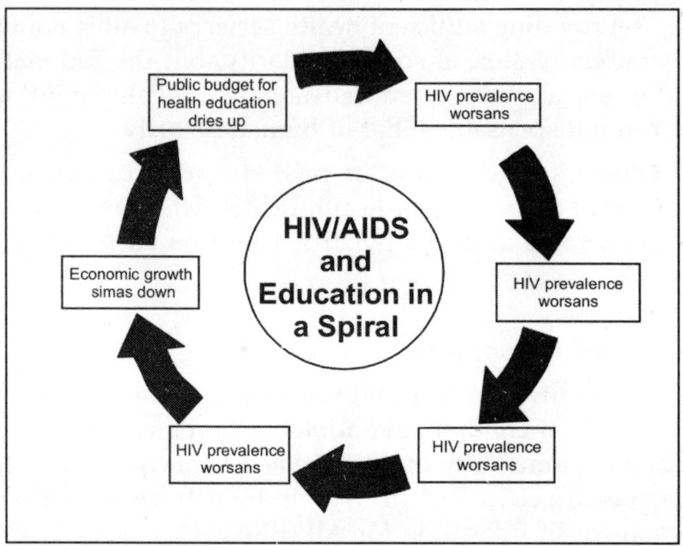

Source: HIV / AIDS and Education: A Toolkit for Ministries of Education, UNESCO Bangkok, 2003.

The FRESH (Focussing Resources on Effective School Health) initiative, launched at the World Education Forum in Dakar in April 2000 with UNESCO, UNICEF, the World Food Programme (WFP), WHO and the World Bank among the early partners, was established to promote the implementation of a core group of cost-effective activities to deliver on the promise of EFA.

The framework proposes four core components of an effective school health and nutrition programme:

- *Policy:* health- and nutrition-related school policies that are non-discriminatory, protective, inclusive, and gender-sensitive;
- *School environment: safe* and psychologically supportive; with access to safe water and separate sanitation facilities for girls, boys, and teachers;

- *Education:* skills-based education, that addresses health, nutrition, HIV prevention, and hygiene is-sues and promotes positive behaviours;
- *Services:* simple, safe, and familiar health and nutrition services that can be delivered cost-ef-fectively in schools and increased access to youth-friendly clinics.

The framework suggests that the programme will be:

- most equitable and cost-effective if all of these components are made available, together in all schools;
- most effective if delivered through strategic partnerships between: health and education sectors (especially teachers and health workers); schools and the community; children and other key stake-holders.

Health and Education for Sustainable Development (ESD)

Health issues, including HIV and AIDS, should be mainstreamed into all aspects of the ESD framework. Effective responses to health challenges, including HIV and AIDS, require approaches that are holistic, multi-sectoral, learner-centred, rights-based, culturally sensitive, gender responsive and locally relevant. Traditional education programmes and systems therefore need to be re-oriented:

- Education does not only have academic purposes—it should also enable educators and learners to learn to live healthily in a world with HIV and AIDS and other health risks;
- Educational institutions are not only venues for teaching and learning, but can be centres of support for learners and educators, or promote referrals to such services;
- Policy, management and systems should provide guidance, oversight, coordination, monitoring and evaluation, to ensure an effective, sustainable and institutionalized educational response to health challenges;

- Educational content, curriculum and materials should emphasize value clarification, capacity-development and skills-building to enable learners to adopt caring and supportive attitudes to others and protective and health-seeking behaviours for themselves;
- Learning outcomes should not only address academic performance, but should also be directed to the full development of human potentiality;
- Education is a life-long process and should be available at all levels and in all social contexts (family, school, workplace, community).

A Framework for Considering HIV & AIDS and Quality Education

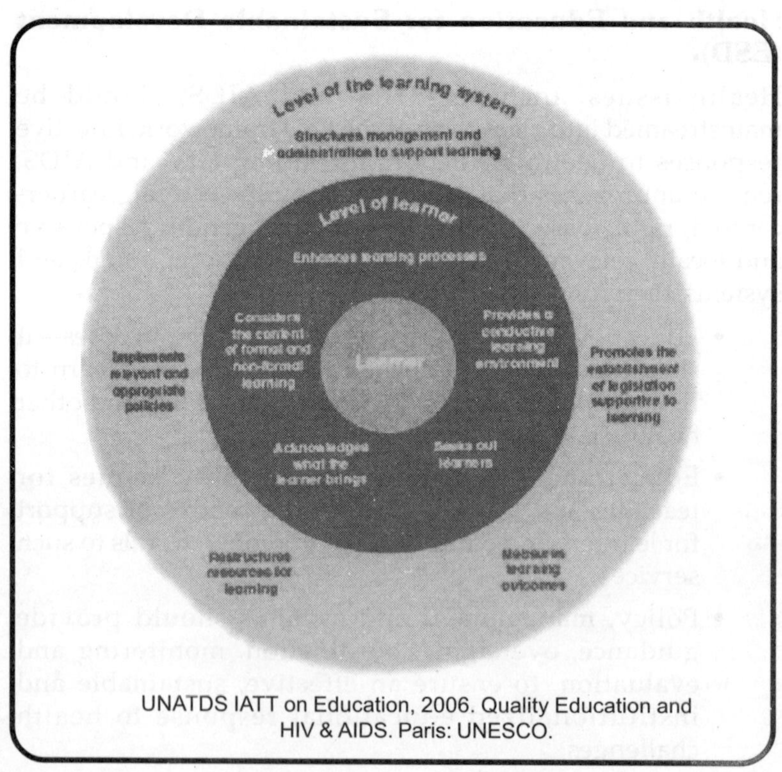

UNATDS IATT on Education, 2006. Quality Education and HIV & AIDS. Paris: UNESCO.

BSD goals and methodologies provide a useful framework for developing effective responses to the causes of ill-health, including HIV and AIDS, through: vision-building and advocacy; consultation and ownership; partnership and networks; capacity-building and training; research and innovations; use of information and communication technologies (ICTs); and monitoring and evaluation.

Similarly, incorporating health issues into the ESD framework makes education more relevant and responsive and interesting to the learners, thereby improving the outcome and quality of education.

Engagement in learning, reflecting and debating on the broader issues which impact on health, such as poverty, gender inequality, the environment, would help learners develop responsible attitudes and behaviours for a sustainable future.

Workshop on AIDS, Health and ESD

The workshop is co-organized by UNESCO and the World Bank with the following objectives:

- Positioning health, including HIV and AIDS, higher on the agenda of sustainable development and ESD;
- Developing a better understanding of the essential contribution of school health responses to SD/ESD, and vice versa;
- Taking stock of DESD implementation, with a par-ticular focus on health, including HIV and AIDS and sustainable development—good practice and evidence; and
- Fostering reflections on strategic direction, priorities for action and partnership modalities for the second half of the DESD.

The workshop will lead the participants to reflect on why and how existing education systems and programmes should/

can be re-oriented towards better responding to sustainable development issues, with particular attention to HIV and health. Where ap-propriate, the FRESH framework will be used as an organizing principle. Specific questions to guide the discussions in the workshop would include:

- How do ESD goals and methodologies intersect with major causes of ill health including HIV and AIDS?
- How does the incorporation of health issues in the education sector help improve the relevance and quality of education?
- How can the ESD framework be adjusted to explicitly include the main causes of ill health so as to enhance the ability of the education sector to better contribute to sustainable development?
- What have we done so far and what are the lessons learnt that we can share?
- What strategic direction, action priorities and partnerships would be most appropriate in the field of AIDS, health and sustainable development?
- What is our own role, as an individual, institution or organization, in achieving sustainable global health?

REFERENCES

1. Beasley, M., Valerio, A., Bundy, D.A.P., Drake, L.J. (2008) Education and HIV/AIDS; A Sourcebook of HIV/ AIDS Prevention Program; Volume 2: Sector-Wide Programmes. World Bank, Washington DC.
2. Bonn Call for Action on Promoting Sustainabie Global Health.
3. http://www.ilo.org/public/german/region/eurpro/bonn/download/bonndeclaration_ef.pdf
4. Bundy, D.A.P., Shaeffer, S, Jukes et al. (2006) School-based Health and Nutrition Programmes, Ch. 58 in Jamison, D.T., Breman, J.G., Measham, A.R., Alleyne, G., Claeson, M., Evans, D.B., Jha, P., Mills, A. and Musgrove, P.(eds.) Disease Control Priorities in Developing Countries, Second Edition, The World Bank and Oxford University Press, NY, USA. pp 1091 -1108.

5. Jukes, J, Simmons, S, and Bundy, D. (2008). Education and Vulnerability: The Role of Schools in Protecting Young Women and Girls from HIV in southern Africa. AIDS 22 (supp 4) S41-56.
6. Jukes, M.C.H., Drake, L.J. and Bundy, D.A.P (2007). School Health, Nutrition and Education for All: Levelling the Playing Field. CAB International Publishing, United Kingdom.
7. Kwok-Cho Tang, Don Nutbeam, Carmen Aldinger et al (2008) Schools for Health, Education and Development: A Call for Action. Health Promotion International. http://heapro.oxfordjournals.org/cgi/content/abstract/ dan037 Oxford University Press
8. UNAIDS. 2008. 2008 Report on the Global AIDS Epidemic. Geneva, UNAIDS. http://www.unaids.org/en/KnowledgeCentre/HIVData/GlobalReport/2008/
9. UNESCO. 2008. EDUCAIDS Framework for Action: Towards a Comprehensive Education Sector Response. 2d Edition. Paris, UNESCO. http://unesdoc.unesco.org/images/0014/001473/147360e.pdf
10. UNESCO. 2008. EDUCAIDS Overviews of Practical Resources. Paris, UNESCO. http://unesdoc.unesco.org/images/0015/001584/158428e.pdf
11. UNESCO. 2008. EDUCAIDS Technical Briefs: Towards a Comprehensive Education Sector Response. Paris, UNESCO. http://unesdoc.unesco.org/images/0015/001584/ 158436e.pdf
12. UNESCO, UNICEF, WHO, World Bank. Focussing Resources on Effective School Health (FRESH): http://www.freshschools.org/Pages/default.aspx
13. WHO. 2008. 10 Facts on the Global Disease Burden. Geneva, WHO. http://www.who.int/features/factfiles/globaLburden/ facts/en/index2.html
14. WHO. 2002. Health and Sustainabie Development—Key Health Trends. Geneva, WHO. http://www.who.int/mediacentre/events/HSD_Plaq_ 02.2_Gb_def1.pdf

CHAPTER

Workshop—6

Mainstreaming Biodiversity into Education and Learning

Introduction

Provision of food, fuel and fiber, shelter and building materials, purification of air and water, detoxification of wastes, moderation of floods and droughts, stabilization of climate, control of pests and diseases, as well as cultural and aesthetic benefits: these are just some of the many services that biodiversity, the diversity of genes, species, and ecosystems, provides to all forms of life on Earth, including humans. Yet, for most people, biodiversity remains the invisible basis for human existence. Increasingly settled in urban settings, the global community is largely unaware of the extent to which their economic, social and cultural well-being is founded on strong, resilient ecosystems, landscapes and seascapes which are themselves buttressed by a rich diversity of genes and species. For those communities that directly rely on biodiversity for their livelihoods, short-term considerations may obscure the impacts of their practices on the capacity of ecosystems to provide essential services on the long-term.

In both cases, this lack of awareness leads to practices that overexploit natural resources and harm biodiversity. Raising awareness of the critical role that biodiversity plays in ensuring environmental sustainability, economic prosperity and social and cultural well-being will contribute to the enhancement and/or the development of sustainable development actions, including ways of organizing thoughtful consumption and production behaviours that are sustainable from local to global levels.

People are willing to take the steps to engage in a life long learning process that will allow them to live in a way that will ensure a sustainable future including saving biodiversity. ESD can provide the values, competencies, knowledge and skills for citizens to realize this process.

During the workshop, participants will engage in group exercises to reflect on the following concepts, linked to the objectives of the Conference:

- *Objective 1:* "Why is ESD relevant?" Participants will reflect on how ESD is a key approach for the promotion of the conservation and sustainable use of biodiversity.
- *Objective 2:* "What can we learn from each other?" Discussions and activities will promote the sharing of how people experience biodiversity, and how it contributes to the identity of communities
- *Objective 3:* "What have we achieved so far, what are the lessons learned?" Participants will share the ways in which biodiversity has already been mainstreamed into different contexts of learning.
- *Objective 4:* "Where do we go from here?" The discussions will culminate in the development of recommendations/guidance for action plans focussed on mainstreaming biodiversity into concrete thematic settings and their integration into ESD plans overall.

Workshop Structure and Organization

The workshop will be structured around three sets of questions, which will be explored through a *variety* of group exercises:

1. Understanding biodiversity and its place in ESD
2. Bringing biodiversity into contexts of learning
3. Action for a sustainable future: experiences with biodiversity

Understanding biodiversity and its place in ESD

A sustainable relationship between human communities and the biodiversity upon which they rely is the cornerstone of a sustainable future. Understood by scientists and resource managers, the concept of biodiversity and its relationship to human well-being however remains opaque and intangible for many. The Millennium Ecosystem Assessment (http:// www. millenniumassessment.org/en/index.aspx) identified the ways that human well-being is founded on the services provided by ecosystems and biodiversity.

Mainstreaming biodiversity into education and learning processes requires that people begin to recognize the relationship between biodiversity and human well-being and reflect on how this is exemplified in every day life. Participants will discuss the following concepts:

- What is biodiversity? How do we understand it in our own contexts ?
- Why is it important for humans and for sustainable development?
- How is biodiversity conservation, sustainable use and the equitable sharing of benefits from the use of genetic resources linked to the goals of ESD?

Bringing Biodiversity into learning contexts

Formal: Formal education systems around the world are continually asked to include a range of social issues in their curricula. At the same time, a concern for the loss of biodiversity and the ethical issues sur-rounding its sustainable use remains central to ESD. Therefore the goal is to infuse key biodiversity messages into the pursuit of a more sustainable future and engage formal education on this basis. Because the conservation and sustainable use of biological diversity is impacted by the activities of many government bodies, the broader context of government policies and commitments in any given country need to be clearly identified and effectively communicated.

Non-formal: People are always learning. They learn from observing others; they learn from their parents; they learn from media; they learn in the workplace; they learn through their own life experiences. Non-formal learning providers support this 'everyday' learning by offering structured and free-choice opportunities for people to explore ideas, to satisfy curiosity, to gain information and skills, and to improve their quality of life. The goal is to identify ways that biodiversity is being explored by these communities and encourage sharing of experiences.

On the basis of the above, participants share their experiences in mainstreaming biodiversity concepts and principles into formal and non-formal contexts of learning. The focus will be on ways to engage different actors including: educational ministries; teachers and students; NGOs, the media and the private sector.

Thematic working groups: Action for a sustainable future—experiences with biodiversity

Taking the principles elaborated in the first two themes as a point of departure, workshop participants will create action plans for including biodiversity into ESD for specific themes:

Using Ecosystem Services Sustainably : The drivers of biodiversity loss: habitat destruction and fragmentation; pollution; invasive alien species; climate change; over-exploitation of resources, are strongly related to unsustainable patterns of consumption by individuals and groups. This group will explore how ESD can contribute to changing practices and attitudes towards more sustainable practices.

Training the Biodiversity Managers of the Future

Management of biodiversity and sustainable production requires a particular set of skills. For example, a body of trained taxonomists is required to understand ecosystem functioning. Resource managers need to be trained in the relationship between the technical and social aspects of biodiversity conservation. ESD can contribute by making opportunities available for societies to train people in these skills. This group will create the framework through which societies can identify the required skills and values.

Cities and Biodiversity

Urban populations rely on biodiversity, whether it is that which is proximate to their surroundings, or the ecosystems which encircle our cities. Urban centres are also places where sustainable patterns of consumption and production can be fostered. This group will explore strategies that cities can use to promote biodiversity protection and encourage sustainable development.

Biodiversity and Cultural Diversity

The rich diversity of life on Earth encompasses not only biological, but also cultural diversity, including variety of practices, traditions, languages, artistic expressions, and belief, value and knowledge systems, which are rooted in and depend on specific aspects of biodiversity. Recognizing that biological diversity is intimately linked to cultural diversity and that together these two forms of diversity hold the key to sustainable development, this group will explore the ways of linking the issues of cultural and biological diversity in the context of ESD and in particular by focussing on integration of the following aspects in education and learning processes:

- cultural values if biodiversity (spiritual, aesthetic, inspirational, recreational and educational values);
- diversity of cultural practices impacting biodiversity and vice versa (use of local food systems and traditional medicine, rituals associated with natural cycles, conservation of sacred sites, eco-tourism);
- diversity of knowledge systems (including local and indigenous traditional knowledge systems, citizen science, and other forms of knowledge).

Moving Forward

The workshop will conclude with a set of recommendations on integrating biodiversity into ESD. These will be based on the dialogue of lessons learned and best practices, that emerges from the working groups. Particular attention will be paid to the ways that biodiversity is part of the goals of ESD.

CHAPTER

Workshop—8

The Economic Pillar of Sustainable Development *Educational Approaches*

Sustainable development is development that meets the needs of the present without compromising the ability of future generations to meeting their own needs.

The World Commission on Environment and Development, Our Common Future

(The Brundtland Report), 1987

Eradicating poverty is the greatest global challenge facing the world today and an indispensable requirement for Sustainable development, particularly for developing countries.

The Plan of Implementation of the Johannesburg World Summit on Sustainable Development, 2002

The concept of Sustainable development must be understood in terms of human needs, rights and responsibility towards the environment as well as in terms of solidarity—between generations and between communities across nations. We must take a holistic approach to the three pillars of sustainable development—economic, social and environmental development. Poverty reduction cannot be delinked from promoting human rights and dignity, building just and peaceful society, and management of the natural resources and the environment. Our thinking and actions tend to remain compartmentalized too often, focusing on one or another of these goals. Achieving MDG 7 on environmental sustainability is vital to reaching the other MDGs on poverty, health and gender equality.

Globally, the extent of poverty remains massive, as half of the world's people live on less than 2 per day. Inequalities between and within countries are extremely high and in many cases rising. The ratio between the incomes of the richest 20 per cent of the world's population to the poorest 20 per cent was 30 to 140 years ago. Today it is 90 to 1. Today, the consumption expenditure in an average African household is 20 per cent less than it was 25 years ago.

On an operational level, the concept and practice of sustainable development must be focused on the fight against poverty. We can continue to talk about further conceptual refinement of the three pillars of sustainable development, but it is necessary to use our energy to take the bull by the horns and address the root cause of the unstable and unsustainable global development. By integrating environmental considerations into the struggle against global poverty, and vice versa, the chances of achieving meaningful progress will substantially increase. At least five aspects of this integrated approach deserve attention.

(a) Marginalisation and disparity and claiming a stake for all in economic and social development, As mentioned above, the vulnerable poor, the large marginal and disadvantaged populations, have to be given a stake in sustainable development. Key elements in this effort are empowerment of people at the local level in designing and achieving poverty reduction; access to productive assets, capital and technology for the poor, microfinance being a widely used instrument; and social safety net and economic support to the ultra-poor,

those who are ineligible even for microfinance, in order to enhance their capabilities to access capital and technology. Development NGOs have played an important role in carrying out economic initiatives for the poor.

Effects of climate change show that poor people are most likely to be the first victims and the greatest sufferers of environmental degradation. The poor are more vulnerable than others to environmental hazards and environment-related conflicts and least able to cope with them when they occur. They, as noted, also tend to be most dependent on the natural environment and direct use of natural resources, and are therefore most severely affected by environmental degradation and lack of access to natural resources.

Issues that the workshop may address: Accepting and recognising that the state and public policy have to provide the lead and set the framework for action to protect the vulnerable groups and assist them to cope with short-term and longer term environmental hazards, do NGOs have a comparative advantage over public agencies in serving marginal and disadvantaged groups? In a framework of public private partnership and corporate social responsibility, what role can the private sector play? What institutional mechanisms and processes can help empowerment of the poor, enable the poor to organize for self-help and assist them to expand their capabilities? What mechanisms exist to assess the effects of climate change on vulnerable groups and geographical areas?

(b) Coping with the feminization of poverty. Women make up two thirds of the world's poorest people, are more likely than men to be poor, mal-nourished and illiterate, usually have less access to medical care, property ownership, and employment, and are far less likely than men to be politically active.

Women are the first to encounter the effects of ecological stress, because they must walk farther to get wood for cooking and heating, to search for clean water and to find new sources of food. The responsibility for rearing children and ensuring sufficient resources to meet their needs for nutrition, health care and schooling falls upon the mother. Women's lives have been inextricably linked to use of the natural resources in traditional society. Economic and technological development and expansion of economic opportunities have often tended to alter the symbiotic relationship and added new stress both on women's life and on the natural environment. (See Sylvia Chant, "Re-visiting the 'feminisation of poverty' and the UNDP gender indices: what case for a gendered poverty index?" UNDP, March 2006.)

The questions that must be asked: Why are women particularly vulnerable; what are the social, cultural and economic roots which persist and must be challenged? What are the specific vulnerabilities of women in particular social, economic, cultural and ecological contexts? What institutional mechanisms are there (or not there) to identify and deal with these? How are women's vulnerabilities recognized in the existing policies and programmes to combat poverty and disparity?

(c) Promoting sustainable production and consumption in the context of poverty reduction. Roughly five per cent of the people of the world in North America enjoys one-third of the world's economic output. On the other hand, one-third of the world's population in China and India can lay claim on only six per cent of the world's economic output. Arguably, the central point of debate on sustainability is whether the pattern of consumption and production in North America and Europe is sustainable for the majority of the world outside the privileged enclave. Another way of posing this question—Is it responsible for the developing world to aspire to emulate and aim to achieve the pattern of production and consumption of North America and Europe? If not, is there an alternative development path that the developing countries need to find and follow, while protecting and promoting the rights, dignity and well-being of all human beings? And what are the moral,

ethical and enlightened self-interest imperatives for the rich countries of the industrial world? (See David Korten, *The Great Turning: From Empire to Earth Community,* 2003)

(d) Globalization-winners, losers and threats to sustainable development Winners and losers from the inexorable forces of globalization are determined by whether people live in the global north or in urban and developed parts of a country, whether they are skilled and educated, whether people have acquired the capacity to adjust to change and new situations easily, whether they possess assets, gender and ethnic status of people, and such factors over which people have little control (Paul Streeten, *Globalization: Threat or Opportunity?,* Copenhagen Business School Press, 2001.) Globalization induced improvements in a nation's standard of living also can promote women's status and raise household income, education, nutrition and life expectancy, while lowering birthrates. The key issues clearly are: How to discern the factors which create the winners and losers, identifying the vulnerable groups affected by these factors; how to determine the conditions and actions that would reduce the vulnerability of people; how to promote and support the creation of these conditions and enable people to engage in these actions.

(e) Developing learning and knowledge network and technology for sustainable development within the framework of lifelong learning.

The argument for a central position of the knowledge network and lifelong learning in the national development agenda is that it can contribute in important ways to meeting the challenges of the modern world both for individuals and societies. These challenges as articulated in development priorities and aspiration of societies have to find a place in the curriculum, learning objectives, educational methodology, and in expanding learning opportunities for all. (M. Ahmed, *Adult Learning and Education: Asia Pacific Synthesis for the Global Report,* UNESCO Institute of Lifelong Learning, Hamburg, 2008)

Establishing the relevance of the educational activities for individuals and society, designing the activities accordingly, implementing these to realize the outcomes, and evaluating if indeed the outcomes and, ultimately the desired impact, have been produced are neither one well-defined task, nor can it be the job of one central agency. There are questions of objectives and priorities in programmes, designing curricula and materials, and assessing outcome and impact of a multitude of activities. Major common development challenges stand out:

(i) Fighting poverty, with the largest concentration in the world of people in extreme poverty in South Asia and Sub-Saharan Africa;

(ii) Promoting sustainable development; life and live-lihood of large numbers of people in the island nations and coastal areas of several countries being under threat, and other aspects of the fragile environment affecting seriously people in all countries; and

(iii) Building participatory democracy and the democratic polity, as people in all countries aspire to build a secure future for themselves and for future generations, with peace, harmony, justice and human dignity.

What do these goals mean in educational terms, and how do these blend with or are balanced with other important concerns in each society? Without being prescriptive and not attempting to decide what each country, and to a degree each community and the learners themselves should decide, how can experiences be shared among countries and lessons are learned about how the complex dynamics work out?

In addressing the knowledge aspects of the identified economic challenges, the workshop will probe the status, trends and innovative initiatives in this respect and indicate the way forward. The action points to be examined at the workshop will include establishing or strengthening learning and knowledge network and linkages, improving quality of teaching-leaning and bringing the ESD perspective into educational content and method; overcoming the digital divide; and promoting the achievement of EFA goals and MDGs—all in relation to poverty reduction.

CHAPTER

Workshop—9

UNESCO Biosphere Reserves as Learning Sites for Integrating Local and Global Sustainability Issues

Background

Biosphere reserves, nominated by national governments and recognized under UNESCO's Man and the Biosphere (MAB) Programme since 1976, are areas of terrestrial, coastal and marine ecosystems established to promote and demonstrate harmonious and sustainable interactions between biodiversity conservation and socio-economic well being of people, through research, education, monitoring, capacity building and participatory management. There are 531 biosphere reserves in 105 countries in the World Network of Biosphere Reserves. Education, training and learning are key elements of biosphere reserves involving various stakeholders, from public administrators, local communities, businesses, scientists to children. During the next 5 years of the United Nations Decade of Education for Sustainable Development (UNDESD), the MAB Programme aims at enhancing the role of *biosphere reserves as learning sites for sustainable development and* build partnerships that will demonstrate that deliberation and dialogue among stakeholders is a necessary condition for sustainable development judgements and decisions aimed at harmonizing between the often conflicting needs of biodiversity conservation, climate change mitigation and adaptation and socio-economic and cultural well being of communities.

Objective

The objective of the workshop is to bring together various stakeholders, including biosphere reserve managers, decision-makers, researchers, universities and UNESCO Chairs, who have succeeded in using the biosphere reserve as a platform for mobilizing local, national and global partnerships for sustainable development. The workshop aims at enhancing sharing of experience and practices of local involvement and engagement from a variety of actors who found innovative and creative ways for working together. These experiences and processes are source of learning, in involving key actors and for building partnerships and social networks critical for sustainability thinking and action.

On Day 1, the international partnerships between two or more biosphere reserves will be presented to share the experiences and knowledge in contributing towards sustainability issues and addressing problems through collaboration at local, national and global levels. On Day 2, participants will discuss and generate a draft strategy for demonstrating the role of biosphere reserves as learning sites for sustainable development in the context of DESD (2009-2014), taking into consideration ESD implementation plan for UNESCO where the MAB Secretariat takes the leadership for issues linked to ecosystems and livelihood, the Madrid Action Plan (MAP) for biosphere reserves (2008-2013) and UNESCO Medium Term Strategy.

Programme

DAY 1 : TUESDAY, 31 MARCH, 15:00-18:00	
15:00-15:05 (5 min)	**Opening by Facilitator**
15:05:15:20 (15 min)	**Workshop purposes and objectives** Mr. Natarajan Ishwaran (UNESCO-MAB)
15:20-15:40 (20 min)	**Presentation 1:** Rhon (Germany) and Kruger to Canyon (South Africa) Biosphere Reserves Ms Doris Pokorny (Germany) Ms Mirjam de Koning (South Africa)
15:40-16:00 (20 min)	**Presentation 2:** Building biosphere reserve partnerships and learning from each other Mr. Djaffaour Tiomoko (Benin) Ms Dominique Potvin (Canada) Ms Valerie Meyer (France)
16:00-16:20 (20 min)	**Presentation 3:** Cat Ba Biosphere Reserve (Vietnam) and the School of Integrative Systems, University of Queensland (Australia) Mr Nguyen Hoang Tri (Vietnam) Mr Ockie Bosch (Australia)
16:20-16:40 (20 min)	**Presentation 4:** University of Belem (Brazil) and Urdaibai Biosphere Reserve (Spain) Mr. Luis Aragon (Brazil) Ms Miren Onaindia (Spain)
16:40-16:55 (15 min)	**Break**
16:55-18:00 (65 min)	**Working Group Session**
DAY 2 : WEDNESDAY, 1 APRIL, 11:00-13:00	
11:00-11:05 (5 min)	**Opening by the Facilitator** Ms Dominique Povtin

11:05-11:15 (10 min)	**Synthesis of Day 1 discussions**
11:15-11:25 (10 min)	**Lessons lernt and future prospect** Mr. Natarajan Ishwaran
11:25-11:40 (15 min)	**MAB and WNBR-African links to Global Agendas** H.E. Mr. Henri Djombo, Chair, MAB/ICC Minister, Forest Economy, Republic of Congo
11:40-11:55 (15 min)	**Environmental Education and Education for Sustainability** Mr Kartikeya Sarabhai, CEE, India
11:55-12:30 (35 min)	**Working Group Session**
12:30-13:00 (30 min)	**Conclusions, recommendations and the way forward**

Output

The workshop will generate a strategic outline for generating case studies and other pedagogic and learning materials for demonstrating the role of biosphere reserves as learning sites for sustainable development during the last five years of UNDESD (2009-2014), in co-operation with the ESD Secretariat, UNESCO and a range of public and private sector partners in all parts of the world. The strategic outline nd other conclusions and recommendations of the workshop will be used to develop proposals to the UNESCO Executive Board and the General Conference scheduled to meet in UNESCO, Paris, during September-October 2009 for using the World Network of Biosphere Reserves as a learning platform for sustainable development.

CHAPTER

Workshop—10

The Role of the Private Sector in ESD

The private sector has a strong tradition of training employees to improve competitiveness. As companies take on a broader role in society, they have extended their influence to other types of education and training. This includes learning at the primary, secondary, tertiary and community levels through both formal and informal channels. On the occasion of the DESD, this workshop aims to better understand the rationale and roles of the private sector in education for sustainable development and education about sustainable development. We will look at the boundaries of business responsibility and the role of government and civil society, with a focus on exploring different modalities of engagement and how to ensure win win partnerships. This background paper outlines some initial thinking on the above.

We live in a world that is increasingly shaped by sustainable development issues. There is no doubt that globalization and opening up of markets and trade have created tremendous economic growth. However, the wealth generated has not been evenly distributed either between countries or within countries, nearly 4 out of 5 people in the world still live on less than $11 per day.

Poverty and inequality is just the tip of the iceberg. The link between energy and climate impacts is becoming increasingly visible. Population growth and rising standards of living will trigger will double or triple energy demand in the coming decades, and water and ecosystems are being degraded or used unsustainably according to the Millennium Ecosystems Assessment, services that business relies on. We are therefore undermining our resources, our people and our societies unless we take the issue of sustainable development seriously.

The business link

These are just some of the challenges the business sector faces, but they demonstrate the inextricable link between business and society in a world estimated to reach nine billion people in 2050. Business leaders increasingly recognize their company's future success depends on how well they address these challenges and how well they understand sustainable development. There are clear business benefits to a Sustainable approach, and weaknesses in environmental, social or health-related performance can present great risks for a company. Sustainable development policies and procedures allow a company to stay 'ahead of the game' as it is anticipating these risks. Sustainable business practices can increase operational efficiency and profitability while improving the environmental and social performance of a company such as eco-efficiency, innovation and safety. A focus on sustainable development will lead to both the development of new markets and increased value in enhancing products, services and brands with positive environmental and social properties.

Where does Education for Sustainable Development (ESD) fit into all of this?

Education is a key pillar of sustainable development. There is a positive correlation between the literacy rate of a country and economic and human development. Education is a key factor in empowering the poorest people to improve their socio-economic situation. Equally, education plays an important role in gender equality and strengthening the social and economic situation of girls and women. In the context of ESD, as described in Chapter 36 of *Agenda 21*, ESD (education for/about sustainable development) has four major focus areas: (1) improve basic education; (2) reorient existing education to address sustainable development; (3) develop public understanding, awareness; and (4) training. The private sector has a role to play in all of these areas.

Improving basic education and reorienting existing education

The onus for improving education tends to fall on national governments, with the help of donors, but companies can and should get involved. Corporations can engage with governments through multi-stakeholder partnerships to support the educational infrastructure, including administrative and project management training and support.

A global meta-review of 12 multi-stakeholder partnerships in education (MSPE) initiatives (Alexandra Draxler, Jan 2008) by Partnerships for Education, a joint initiative between UNESCO and the World Economic Forum to research and catalyze the use of MSPEs on a global level has found that the involvement of private sector to help achieve a country's national education sector plan has the comparative advantage of:

- Making education relevant to the economy
- Innovation—in education and more widely
- Educational programmes can readily be targeted to specific groups
- Improved technological and financial management techniques
- Improving the overall learning environment

Through engagements with Jordan, Rajasthan, and Egypt since 2003, the World Economic Forum Global Education Initiative has developed a country education model (Tom Cassidy, October 2007) to facilitate the government's engagement with private sector and other key education stakeholders in developing win-win partnerships.

The GEI Model of Effective Partnership Initiatives for

4. Leadership, Governance and Decision-making

Programme Management Office

1. Core Values & Objectives
2. Vision, Goals & Objectives
3. Organizational Readiness

5. Management & Implementation
6. Planning
7. Communications
8. Resource Mobilization

9. **Schools Communities**
1. Principles
2. Teachers
3. Students

10. **Partners**
1. ICT Partners
2. Other Partners

12. Results

11. Monitoring and Evaluation

In reviewing the lessons learned where government has partnered with the private sector in education, several items stand out:

- Multi-stakeholder partnerships initiatives can be very effective providing sufficient care is taken and there is early agreement on fundamental principles
- Multi-partner initiatives must be very well and systemically managed with guidelines and legal frameworks in place
- An assessment of needs and desired results should be the first step

- MSPEs may not reduce costs, and there is may additionally be a need to fund the unforeseen
- Leadership and management teams must include a balanced representation of stakeholders
- Changing what goes on in schools, and particularly changing teaching practices in classrooms, is a much more complex and challenging undertaking than partners often believe.
- Teachers and principals are at the heart of the change process and must be involved actively in their design and implementation.
- Sustained partner involvement should not be taken for granted.
- Monitoring and evaluation with transparent reporting must be given much greater attention in all such initiatives
- Good partnerships and partners should not be taken for granted.

Developing awareness and building capacity

To gain business value, sustainability must be adopted as a core feature of corporate practice—from supply chain, R&D, to codes of conduct to energy efficiency, which mergers and acquisitions, to transparency and reporting. Yet despite progress, few companies have the relevant leadership and capabilities in place to deliver on business and sustainability priorities, with limited buy in from most parts of the corporation. Companies are therefore exploring how to inform, train, equip, direct, motivate and support employees in sustainable development. Sustainability requires new knowledge, skills and values to allow managers to balance profitability with stakeholder interests and social and environmental realities. A critical mass of employees with the basic comprehension of sustainable development is required to achieve sustainable literacy, and these concepts need to be integrated into a range of disciplines such as marketing, finance, strategy, supply chain management and human resources.

This does not imply that learning should be uniform. Specialist responsibilities—for example to assess labour conditions in global supply chains will normally be assigned to particular individuals and will require specific training and development. However, developing three generic capabilities will help business to address its strategic goals and generate long-term value:

- In an increasingly interdependent world, it is critical to be aware of the local and global context in which companies are operating in;
- Sustainable development requires a long-term view—it is about meeting our needs today while still being able to hand over the planet to the future generations;
- Companies must continually enhance their work-force's skills to respond to the emerging demands of customers, investors and society. Part of this is understanding why a stakeholder approach is essential to an organization's long-term approach and who and how to consult.

To best learn about sustainable development issues, especially in the private sector where time is of the essence, many companies are developing in-house training programmes. This often involves action learning—putting an employee through an experience, allowing them to experiment and use their judgment to understand the complexity of the topic. Companies also make use of executive education programmes for senior management. These programmes are increasingly integrating sustainable development issues into leadership, strategy and ethics to equip executives to think and manage more effectively in a changing business world.

For large corporations, investing in BSD education and training can:

- Create a healthier, better trained, more qualified work force
- Create a larger pool of labour locally with the appropriate skill sets and knowledge to meet the particular requirements of the corporation
- Lead to improved capacity and performance of local suppliers
- Strengthen the business licence to operate through participation in local enterprise development and the development of vocational training programmes
- Make an important contribution to curriculum development, particularly at secondary and tertiary education levels, ensuring that it stays relevant to business needs.

CHAPTER

Workshop—11

Media as Partners for ESD

Introduction

The new concept of education for sustainable development reflects the report established in 1990 by the World Commission on Environment and Development, at the time under the presidency of Ms. Gro Harlem Brundtland, former Prime Minister of Norway. This has taken shape over the course of the last ten years defining development as that which "satisfies the needs of the present without compromising the opportunity for future generations to satisfy the needs of their own".

The sustainable development agenda is vast. It covers issues ranging from the depletion of the ozone layer to child labour, deforestation (which plays a role in climate change), education, globalisation, etc. Education has proven to be important at every level, allowing individuals to acquire knowledge they do not have and reinforce knowledge they have already gained. In fact, the need for education varies from one region to another, from one population to another, from one culture to another and from one age to another. However, all human beings need education.

The importance of education in confronting human environment problems already highlighted by the United Nations Conference on the Human Environment in Stockholm in 1972 was recalled ten years later at the Earth Summit in Rio de Janeiro. The World Summit on Sustainable Development in Johannesburg in 2002 identified links between the environment and the economy and reaffirmed the commitment of different countries of the world to promote sustainable development and to improve the skills of the individual. The United Nations General Assembly therefore declared the period 2005-2014 the United Nations Decade of Education for Sustainable Development. "The founding vision of ESD is a world in which everyone has the opportunity to benefit from education and to acquire the values, behaviour and lifestyles necessary for a sustainable future and a positive transformation of society." Hence the need to have the media as partners.

By nature, the presence of public, private, commercial, alternative, national and community media results in plurality. The diverse contents give different social groups the opportunity to identify themselves with the media. Information circulates better (notably when tackling issues of public interest) when the media belongs to different entities.

Producing and broadcasting programmes through the media has a very high cost, called 'first-copy costs'. To cover these costs, media producers often have a strong incentive to produce content for the largest number of consumers, presenting material that serves larger audiences with a view to attract the advertisers. Therefore the pure economic characteristics of media markets lead natural market forces to discriminate against the preferences of minorities—racial, ethnic, and any other relatively small groups whose tastes in media differ from the majority's.

The media has considerable power which can be explained by the way it influences opinion. It is a source of informal education for all generations and all social classes.

As it turns out, interest in doing this is relatively weak everywhere; as a result, a large number of citizens are deprived of an independent voice. The need to acquire crucial information, political, economic or otherwise, is therefore far from being satisfied, even if the wheels of the market are still turning.

It is thus important to have an exchange between decision-makers and training sessions designed for journalists and professionals involved in public communication on education for sustainable development, during which they learn necessary techniques for effective communication of the issue.

The questions which the workshop "Media, Education for Sustainable Development Partners" will attempt to answer will deal with problems in practising journalism and the participation of the media in education for sustainable development.

Are the media really partners or is it necessary to ask them to be partners? How do we do this?

Workshop objectives

The workshop aims to highlight the importance of a favourable environment which will allow journalists and other media professionals to consider and deal with issues linked to ESD.

This is in accordance with the following objectives of the World Conference on Sustainable Development:

1. To highlight ESD's essential contribution to achieving good quality education;
2. To promote international exchange of ESD;
3. To make the first assessment of the implementation of the Decade of Education for Sustainable Development;
4. To develop strategies for continuing it.

Discussions

Workshop participants are invited to take an active part in workshop discussions in order to answer the following important questions through the exchange of opinion:

- Why involve the media in education for sustainable development?
- Are they really partners or is it necessary to ask them to be partners?
- How can the media be made more effective in dealing with issues linked to education for sustainable development?

Work groups

This workshop will be made up of four work groups according to the following four sub-topics:

Group I

Education for sustainable development by the media *(analysis of the current situation): this group will evaluate the quality of the media's work as regards education for sustainable development.*

Group II

Handling of ESD issues by the media in different regions of the world *(similarities and differences)—this group's task will be to carry out a comparative study of media in the north and south with a view to establishing a common interactive policy. Different cultures do in fact influence the way in which issues are appreciated and approached. How can cultural differences be overcome and adapted to world politics?*

Group III

Development of the media's essential contributions to ESD *to ensure sustainability of development—despite recorded efforts during the first half of the decade of education for sustainable development,* *much remains to be done to improve the quality of education at all levels. Define the mechanisms which will help answer any questions which have not yet been resolved.*

Group IV

Classify or prioritise the initiatives to be carried out*—there are of course many initiatives to be carried out, but they do not carry the same importance everywhere. It is important to adapt specific policies according to need.*

Expected results

The expected results of this workshop are:

- To have harmonised the understanding of the notion of ESD by the media in different regions of the world;
- Good national policies consisting in making information available in real time;
- Awareness by journalists of their profession and promotion of their work by stakeholders;
- To have encouraged the partnership between the media, formal and informal education institutions and other stakeholders in ESD. *Listing priority initiatives to be carried out within this partnership in relation to the Millennium Development Goals.*

The results of this workshop, one of twenty-two workshops making up the world conference in Bonn, will firstly be covered in the workshop's report and then in the final report of the world conference in Bonn.

CHAPTER

Workshop—12

ESD in North-South-South and South-South Partnerships and Development Cooperation

Background

This workshop is looking at creating and achieving effective Partnerships and Development Cooperation which should be taking place globally in order to strengthen the processes of Education for Sustainable development. The workshop is also looking at the processes that are necessary to foster and sustain the partnerships and development cooperation.

The workshop aims to highlight the importance of *a* favourable environment which will allow journalists and other media professionals to consider and deal with issues linked to ESD.

However, it is important to keep in mind the shaping events and imperatives that has brought about ESD.

- Education for Sustainable Development is rooted on UN's concern over *quality of basic education* and *sustainable development,* therefore it is a response to the human-environment-development nexus.[1]

- Using *educational and learning aspects to add focus and relevance* to efforts of Education For All goals, the Literacy Decade, Agenda 21 Chapter 36, the Millennium Development Goals and other global, regional and sub-regional educational efforts.
- *The ESD orientation* involves *integrating* principles, values and practices of sustainable development *into all aspects of education and learning* in order to encourage change in behaviour that will create a more sustainable future in terms of environmental integrity, economic viability, and a just society.[2]
- Global social justice in relation to the education principles and support that are developed and owed to the people in the global village should take acceptance of the *existing contrasts in global influences and principles and local interpretation of those global influences and principles* which cause an axis of tension.[3]
- *Education* is to be understood to take place broadly in formal, non-formal and informal settings and it is supported by various actors.

Partnerships and Development Cooperation

Networks are imbedded in the mutual understanding of the actors, actants; the context in which they operate; the factors that impact on them and their aspirations. This notion is crucial especially in view of the inconsistencies that exist as global agreements get devolved to local policies and local institutional structures. Part of this tension comes from the fact that the concept of sustainable development is at times contested and not clearly defined, and that the lead agencies and implementing agencies are not necessarily aligned from global to local levels[4].

With this in mind, it is therefore crucial to consider that partnerships and cooperation are based on multiple actors, including, formal and non-formal education, and the various levels of education including early childhood, primary and secondary, higher education and vocational training. This is articulated well in Wickenberg[5] when he looked at the actors and actants involved in contributing to the greening of curricula in Europe. These included contribution of the curriculum, the educator and the learner, institutional setting (the school), various levels of government and their line ministries, interested parties like parents, Community-based Organisations and Non-Governmental Organisations, resources and policy.

Role of Networks

Networks are communities of practice that relate and work together in order to achieve meaningful, sustainable and relevant interventions. The value of democratic universality is at the heart of reason why networks are vehicles for intervention. They provide discussion points, evidence gathering and sharing; and dialogue on what works and what does not work. They therefore form aggregative and deliberative nodes and/or webs.

In relation to ESD implementation, there are opportunities to carry out stock taking of what has been attempted and achieved, what are the enabling factors and barriers, and what lessons are being learnt.

Challenges for Partnerships and Development Cooperation ESD in North-South-South & South-South

In deliberating on Partnerships and Development Cooperation in ESD some of the challenges that are worth bearing in mind for include:

- Where we want to go from here;
- forming continuity from previous conferences;

- dealing with the change in the nature of discourse around ESD including establishment and interpretation of ESD with respect to education and learning;
- Understanding and working with current practices in networks including—
  - politics of ESD—the history of exclusion versus the notion of inclusion;
  - Knowledge production—values.
- Merging the processes and structures of formal and non-formal education and learning;
- Support systems and activities of resultant networks.

REFERENCES

1. Lotz-Sisitka, H., Gumede, M., Oiivit L. & Pesanayi, T. 2006. *Partnerships, Networking & ESD in Southern Africa: Supporting Participation in the UN Decade of Education for Sustainable Development.* Howick. SADC REEP.
2. UNESCO. 2005. *International Implementation Scheme of the UN Decade of Education for Sustainable Development.* Paris: UNESCO.
3. Unterhalter, E. 2007. *Gender, Schooling and Global Social Justice.* Routledge Taylor & Francis Group. London.
4. Gumede, M. 2008. *Environmental Education Policy Support in Southern Africa: A Case Story of SADC Regional Environmental Education Programme.* Unpublished Masters Thesis, Rhodes University, South Africa.
5. Wickenberg, P. (2000). *Greening Education in Europe.* Sweden: Lund University.

Workshop—13

Global Responsibilities and Local Realities

Fostering ESD through Institutional Frameworks

Purpose

The focus of the workshop will be on *sharing experiences* in the development of international, regional, national and local institutions to progress the objectives of education for sustainable development, *identifying their relevance* to the achievement of these objectives and *developing recommendations for future actions.*

Background

The United Nations Decade of Education for Sustainable Development (UNDESD) called for an increased emphasis on the role of education in promoting sustainable development. As part of the process of responding to this challenge, there is a need to improve the capacity of individuals, organisations and governments to engage effectively in ESD. This requires not only the education of individual educators in the principles of ESD but also the development and establishment of institutional frameworks to promote ESD at a policy and system level.

In some countries national and regional strategies and frameworks for ESD have been developed to guide coordinated action at sub-national and national level. The Africa region launched the DESD and its regional *Strategy of Education for Sustainable Development for Sub-Saharan Africa* (SSAESD) at the Association for the Development of Education in Africa (ADEA) Biennial meeting (Libreville, Gabon, 27-31 March 2006). The regional strategy for the Asia-Pacific was launched at the Asia-Pacific DESD Regional Launch in Nagoya, Japan, in June 2005. In Europe and North America a regional ESD strategy was prepared under the leadership of the United Nations Economic Commission for Europe (UNECE), and was adopted at the UNECE High-level meeting in Vilnius, Lithuania 2005. The regional strategy document, entitled *"Building Education for Sustainable Development in Latin America and the Caribbean"* was completed in 2007. These regional frameworks are significant steps, in mobilising concerted regional effort and promoting action by informing local institutional frameworks. Furthermore, several initiatives have already been taken at international level by the following: International Agencies (United Nations and other) UNESCO[1], Civil Society and NGO networks, bilateral and multilateral development agencies. The International Implementation Scheme (US) outlines some of the potential partners and their roles in DESD[2].

Issues

Given the global and interconnected nature of sustainable development, there is a need for action on ESD at all levels. While local action is essential, the establishment of frameworks that promote broader cooperation and coordination is vital in order to achieve the degree of societal change required. Integral to such change is cross cutting issues such as Gender, Inclusion, Culture, Traditional Knowledge and Human rights. There is also a need to understand issues of sustainability based on three key areas: educational activities, the role of values in ESD, and the linkages between the Decade and other educational initiatives (MDG's.EFA, and UNLD)[3].

Various questions arise. What frameworks are required? What is in place in different parts of the world? What has been proven to work effectively? How important are different cultural settings in establishing institutional frameworks? How important are institutional arrangements that entail whole-organisation and whole-system approaches? While ESD involves all areas of society, how important is the engagement of national governments in providing leadership for education for sustainable development? How do institutional frameworks enable ESD that will take into account the multiple and diverse indigenous knowledge systems and cultural perspectives? How do institutional ESD frameworks take into account issues of gender, inclusion, culture and human rights? How do countries relate the national and regional frameworks with institutional frameworks? How do we galvanise whole-institutional participation in ESD without duplication? What are the monitoring and evaluation mechanisms needed to assess progress made in fostering ESD through institutional frameworks. What are the recommendations to the conference on future actions in line with the global responsibilities and local realities/challlenges.

Target Group

The target group for this workshop is government and non-government participants who are involved in policy setting and programme implementation at a system and institutional level.

Session Content and Structure

The workshop will provide an opportunity to learn from the experiences of other countries in building ESD capacity through the establishment of institutional frameworks at local, national, regional and international level. The focus will be on knowledge exchange with a view to identifying what institutional frameworks have been shown to work, what gaps exist and what enhancements might be made to achieve better outcomes. Resourcing issues are important but the emphasis will be on identifying the relevance and priority of different frameworks not funding solutions.

The scope of the workshop will cover all forms of education—formal, non-formal and informal—and the role that both government and non-government bodies can play.

Objectives/Expected Outcomes

1. Increased knowledge by participants of various approaches to establishing institutional frame-works aimed at promoting improved education for sustainable development.
2. Appreciation of issues and needs in the establishment of ESD institutional frameworks.
3. Recommendations to the broader conference on future actions.

REFERENCES

1. See more details on UNESCO's role from the document: UN Decade of Education for Sustainable Development (DESD 2005-2014) The First Two Years, http://unes-doc.unesco.org/images/0014/0014/0014086/148650/E.pdf.pdf.
2. See http://unesdoc.unesco.org/images/0015/001540/154093e.pdf.
3. MDG's, EFA and UNLD: Millennium Development Goals, Education For All and United Nations Literacy Decade respectively.

CHAPTER

Workshop—14

Civil Society as Key Players in Education for Sustainable Development (ESD)

> *"The United Nations once dealt only with Governments. By now we know that peace and prosperity cannot be achieved without partnership involving Governments, international organisations, the business community and civil society. In today's world, we depend on each other".*
>
> ***(Former Secretary General Kofi Annan, United Nations)***

Civil Society basically refers to organisations or institutions which are non-economic/non-profit and non-governmental in nature. They have a commitment to working in the field of socio-development issues like rural development, alleviation of poverty, nutrition and health, environment, human rights as well as other common human values.

Civil Society has been recognized as a significant partner and contributor to society. Organisations like the United Nations and the World Bank support formal associations with major civil society organisations. In fact Article 71 of the United Nations Charter establishes arrangements for UN consultations with civil society organisations.

The greatest strengths of civil society are its processes or structures which are essentially less formal. This strength allows for deliberation and discussion of multi-disciplinary views, issues and concerns which are important if it were to expand its role of creating and sharing knowledge gathered by its involvement and engagement with the communities.

Civil Society and ESD

Sustainable Development is a complex and evolving concept requiring learning of the relevant knowledge, tools, skills and attitudes. Such capacity building is not a monopoly of formal academic institutions only. The third estate plays an equally important role, and in some cases even more so.

The World Summit on Sustainable Development established that education is vital in promoting sustainability and a Sustainable future and that it is pertinent to mobilize resources at all levels including Civil Society.

Thus, this workshop aims to:

1. engage participants in discussions on the pivotal role of civil society in ESD;
2. challenge the participants to critically reflect on the role of civil society in capacity building for all age groups through formal, non-formal and informal learning arrangements;

Workshop Approach

There will be no formal presentations, but participants will be engaged in a small groups (10 to a group) leading to discussions in the Plenary. There will be 3 resource persons as well as the workshop coordinator facilitating the activities. Participants will be encouraged to share their experiences to enrich the discussions with practical issues reflecting the realities on the ground.

Key Workshop Questions

1. What has been the role of civil society as a champion and catalyst for ESD?
2. How has civil society influenced mainstream academic institutions on ESD issues, for instance issues like pedagogy, content, etc.?
3. What areas of capacity building on ESD has civil society implemented on its own and in partnership with other sectors (and consider comparative advantage of each arrangement)?
4. Civil society is diverse, what have been the rallying points for ESD for scaling up and what have been points of variance requiring further stakeholder engagement (e.g. ethical/moral, ideological grey areas)?
5. What can civil society do in the next 5 years of DESD to assist in identifying and addressing the gaps between the kind of education still prevailing and that necessary for the transition to sustainable development?

Alignment with Conference Objectives

These questions as well as the approaches used in the workshop will generate discussion around all four conference objectives:

(1) ESD and its essential contribution to quality education

(2) promote international exchange on ESD

(3) carry out stock-taking of DESD implementation

(4) develop strategies for the way ahead.

Expected Outcomes

- A greater appreciation of civil society as a catalyst and champion of ESD.
- Accept that civil society is diverse and that the diversity offers greater value for ESD if properly harnessed.

- Identify newer opportunities from shared experience for civil society to scale up in its implementation of ESD

Programme

9.00	Welcome and Brief Introduction
9.15	Ice-breaking and Experience-sharing (Participants will share their experiences in their own group, with a focus on 'Lessons Learnt' and 'Challenges' that they face in engaging communities/stakeholders on ESD. Each group will appoint a representative to capture the sharing and compile 'common issues/concerns'.
9.45	Carousel Exercise-3 groups tackle questions 1-3.
10.30	Break
11.30	Groups (3) tackle question 4 and present to plenary
12.00	Plenary presentations by 3 groups on question 4
12.30	Workshop rapporteur presents main workshop outcomes to be reported by the Cluster rapporteur to the main conference.
1.00	End

CHAPTER

Workshop—15

From the Margins into the Centre

Establishing ESD in Education Plans and Curricula

Rationale

Increased awareness of the problems of environmental challenges, globalisation and poverty has meant that the concepts of environmental education, global learning, and education in development have recently been given more prominence in education policies.

However, in the past these learning areas sometimes have been pushed to marginal, extracurricular areas such as clubs or other non-compulsory activities, when- and wherever the serious, examinable work was not scheduled. This heritage places a burden on ESD, which, as a fairly recent concept, still has to find its way from the fringes of education programmes into the mainstream.

The challenge is to place ESD in the centre of education by moving into the areas of mainstream education plans and curricula. These areas are the policy, regulatory and operational frameworks of education systems and the syllabuses and curricula at all levels. Since syllabuses and curricula are usually oriented towards and deriving from teaching subjects, and subject teaching makes up for the bulk of time in schools 'spent on task', ESD has to be mainstreamed into subject curricula. But as an approach integrating the pillars of sustainable development, the economic, social and environmental dimension towards sustainability, ESD cannot be restricted to subject domains only, but has to maintain the integrity as a crosscutting learning area.

Thus cross-curricular teaching is an essential component of ESD. Learning in ESD should provide pupils with a future-oriented viewpoint on the increasingly globalised world and the issues affecting the future, which they will then be able to build upon further in the context of lifelong learning. They should acquire basic competencies that correspond to shaping their personal and professional lives and help them to get involved in their own societies and share responsibility in a global setting.

Workshop objectives

The workshop pursues the 4 objectives of the conference:

1. to highlight the essential contribution of Education for Sustainable Development (ESD) to all of education and to achieving quality education;
2. to promote international exchange on ESD;
3. to carry out a stock-taking of DESD implementation;
4. to develop strategies for the way ahead.

The approach of the workshop links ESD to relevant competencies to be developed by learners. The workshop will establish that ESD can provide pupils with guidance for a future in an increasingly globalized world, which they can build upon in the context of lifelong learning. Thus ESD provides a valuable contribution to education in general, (*Objective 1*)

Several inputs into the workshop promote international exchange: The Southern African regional initiative, the Chat of the Worlds and the School Exchange Programme are good practice examples of international exchange, the Programme of International Learning Partnerships is at present being designed to facilitate the South-South, North-South exchange on ESD (*Objective* 2)

The inputs into the workshop reflect the experiences of two countries (Costa Rica and Germany) and one region (Southern Africa). They are part of the ESD implementation within the framework of the Decade. Participants in the workshop will be are asked to reflect on the good practice examples and contribute by sharing their own experiences, (*Objective* 3)

Participants at the workshop will be asked to contribute to the question 'Where do we want to go from here?' (*Objective* 4)

Workshop Content

Apart from providing the opportunity to reflect on the workshop theme 'from the margins to the centre', three areas of good practice from different parts of the world form 'the core' of the workshop.

Costa Rica

The aim of the participation of Costa Rica at the World Conference on Education for Sustainable Development is to share an experience based not only in pedagogical principles but in social, political and cultural views. This has been possible thanks to the collaboration and establishment of alliances with national and international NGOs as well as with other institutions, recognized as 'Collaborators.'

If we understand the curriculum as a social construction that synthesizes a national feeling and aspiration, it has to have a social and cultural foundation, not only a pedagogical one. That is why in Costa Rica two main sources created by consensus are leading all formal and non formal education programmes in this area:

1. The Peace with Nature Initiative (IPN as its acronym stands in Spanish) is a presidential initiative, officially launched by President Oscar Arias on July 6, 2007 and represents a strong political commitment of Costa Rica to achieve sustainable development and to fight environmental degradation both at the national and global levels;
2. National Commitment Towards the Decade on Education for Sustainable Development. It looks for the generation of a change of culture through a comprehensive and holistic approach to ESD that will guarantee that present and future generations of Costa Ricans live together in peace, with social equity, in harmony with themselves, with others and with the environment, without discrimination of gender, race, religion, nationality, culture, age, sexual orientation, different abilities or otherwise.

Germany

Within the frame of the National Action Plan of the ESD-Decade, the Standing Conference of the Ministers of Education and Cultural Affairs of the states in the Federal Republic of Germany and the Federal Ministry of Economic Cooperation and Development have developed a *Cross-Curricular Framework for Global Development Education.* The framework serves the purpose of establishing a cross-curricular Global Development teaching programme, in the context of education for sustainable development, in the curricula of general and vocational schools. The Cross-Curricular Framework is a frame of reference for the development of syllabuses and teaching curricula at school, for designing and checking lessons and extra-curricular activities, as well as for study-area and subject-specific requirements. In addition, it can be relevant for teacher education.

The components of development—society, economy, politics and environment/ecology—are related to school subjects and disciplines. The Cross-curricular framework uses these four components of development as the starting point to structure the complex questions of global development and provide recommendations on how to handle these questions in the classroom. The workshop will provide information on several programmes which contribute to the implementation of the Cross-curricular Framework.

Southern Africa

As part of its contributions towards sustainable development, the Southern African Development Community Environmental Education Programme (SADC REEP) aims to strengthen ESD processes for equitable and sustainable environmental management choices in southern Africa.

SADC REEP has succeeded in establishing an active network involving regional ESD centres, NGOs and networks. It has also forged partnerships with international organisations involved in the ESD processes. These include UNESCO and UNEP. Networking under the SADC REEP provides ESD practitioners from countries where ESD practice is limited or lacking to find colleagues, resources, ideas and support for strengthening and extending these activities. It links these practitioners not only to the programme's immediate contacts and resources, but also to those in the broader networks of which the Programme is a part. For example, participants to the SADC REEP activities such as training programmes and meetings are exposed to other networks in the region where they can benefit from a wider network. These exposures have significant impacts as they not only inform but also enthuse and motivate ESD practitioners.

Workshop Approach and Methodology

The workshop uses the World Cafe methodology. World Cafe is a method, which has worked in the international context.

It is a tool of the personalized knowledge management and offers the possibility of open, creative conservation, with the goal of a better common understanding and solution.

The plenary is divided into seven smaller groups, gathering around tables. A facilitator (host) moderates the discussion at each table and will give a brief introduction to the topic. After 40 min. the participants move to the next table. Finally the moderators (hosts) are giving a short presentation of the results to the plenary.

http://www.theworldcafe.com (English website on the method, some materials also in other languages)

Hosts (facilitators) at the seven tables

(1) Justin Lupele, Zambia, SADC-REEP, focus on networking between stakeholders, the regional aproach in Southern Africa www.sadc-reep.org.za.

(2) Claudia Charpentier, Costa Rica, focus on the tertiary sector and ESD plans and curricula.

(3) Robert Schreiber, Hamburg, Focus on school curricula, Geography and ESD http://igu-cge.tamu.edu/ (several declaration).

(4) Insa Sommer, Diisseldorf, Chat of the Worlds, focus on ESD learning communities using the internet www.chatderwelten.de.

(5) Christine Blome, Berlin, ESD and North-South school partnerships—Focus on the development of competencies of ESD via school-partnerships between Germany and developing countries/countries of transition www.ensa-programm.com

(6) Hannes Siege, Bonn, The making and implementation of the Cross-curricular Frame Work, focus on elaboration, test examples, implementation, the national and international dimension (international learning partnerships) www.gc21.de/KMK-BMZ

(7) Alejandrina Mata, Costa Rica, focus on environmental education and ESD in the school system.

CHAPTER

Workshop—16

Teacher Education in the DESD *Review and Directions*

Introduction

The reorienting of teacher education to address sustainability has been identified as one of the most effective ways to promote ESD in educational institutions. Through teacher education institution's work with pre-service and in-service teachers, the potential to reach the world's estimated sixty million teachers is maximised. Teacher education is, therefore, one of the main vehicles through which capacity for implementing ESD can be built.

The workshop will review initiatives in the first half of the DESD, assess the contributions of the DESD to these, identify enabling and challenging factors for enhancing the contributions of the DESD in the next 5 years, and make recommendations for enhancing the quality, relevance and up-take of UNESCO guidelines on teacher education for ESD.

UNESCO Initiatives

The call in 1998 from the United Nations Commission on Sustainable Development work programme in ESD for

UNESCO to develop guidelines for reorienting teacher education to address sustainability was a significant turning point in international action in this field. UNESCO's response to the call was to establish an international network of 30 teacher-education institutions in 28 countries. Teacher educators in these institutions engaged in a four-year process of study, trials and action research to develop a wide range of innovative projects, including:

- Reviewing and revising their existing courses to address sustainability.
- Infusing ESD into other disciplines at under-graduate and graduate level programmes such as agriculture, population education, and consumer education.
- Developing advanced Certificate programmes in ESD for teachers.
- Developing distance education courses in ESD for teachers.
- Developing graduate level programmes for teachers in ESD at Masters' and PhD levels.
- Developing a compulsory ESD course for Masters' programmes in Geographical and Environmental Education.
- Establishing a national ESD professional development consortium.
- Holding institution-wide, national, and international conferences and workshops on ESD.
- Developing community-based off-campus teacher education projects within the inner city to improve the delivery of schooling to undereducated youth.
- Developing link between the faculty of education and the school of business to co-develop professional development programmes on ESD for senior level education administrators.

- Publishing manuals, texts, Web sites, and other sustainability teaching resources for elementary and secondary schools.
- Developing interfaculty exchanges related to ESD among universities.[1]

These teacher educators reflected on their initiatives and distilled a set of over 70 recommendations across eight areas of action. These recommendations have since been published as *The UNESCO Guide-lines and Recommendations for Reorienting Teacher Education to Address Sustainability,* and have featured in many workshops and conferences during the DESD. While they do not provide specific advice on a minimum set of ESD concepts or skills for a teacher education course—perhaps such is not even possible or desirable—they provide a solid base from which we can further explore ways of promoting teacher education and ESD.

UNESCO has also developed a range of materials to support the contributions of teacher education to ESD. These include: *Teaching for a Sustainable World (a)* joint UNESCO-UNEP project[2]); *Learning for a Sustainable Environment* (a UNESCO project that supported an action research network for teacher educators in seventeen Asia-Pacific countries[3]); *Good Practices in ESD in Teacher Education Institutions* (Good Practices No1-2007, UNESCO Education Sector); the UNESCO multimedia teacher education programme, *Teaching and Learning for a Sustainable Future*[4]. This programme provides over 100 hours of self-study for teacher and student teachers. Twenty-five highly interactive workshops provide knowledge and skills across four areas of ESD: Curriculum Rationale, ESD Across the Curriculum, Teaching Interdisciplinary Themes, and Teaching and Learning Strategies for ESD. Available as both a website and a CD-Rom, *Teaching and Learning for a Sustainable Future* is especially valuable in providing in-service teacher education on a self-study basis when it is very difficult and expensive to bring teachers together for professional development. The programme was developed as a demonstration project to encourage widespread adaptation for local use. Accordingly, *Teaching and Learning for a Sustainable Future* has been translated and/or adapted for use by teacher educators in Southern Africa, China, Japan and Mexico with plans for Arabic and Slovak versions. The English version is being updated for the 2009 mid-Decade conference in Bonn.

Other Initiatives

These projects reflect a wide range of significant teacher education projects in many parts of the world, such as: the *Sustainable Teacher Environmental Education Project (STEEP)* in Jamaica[5]; the *School Development through Whole School Approaches to Sustainability Education: The Sustainability Education in European Primary Schools (SEEPS)* (a European Union pre-service teacher education project) as well as the EU and OECD in-service teacher education projects, *School Development through Environmental Education (SEED)*[6] *and Environment and School Initiatives* (E/VS/J.[7] The Centre for Environmental Education (CEE) in India has also collaborated with the Commonwealth of Learning to develop a Diploma in Environmental Education for teachers, called the "Green Teacher" course[8] while teacher education is also a key aspect of the *MESA (Mainstreaming Environment and Sustainability into African Universities) Partnership,* coordinated by UNEP.[9]

Despite this expanding list of initiatives in many parts of the world, the area of teacher education and ESD is remarkably under-researched. There is much anecdotal evidence, however, that ESD has not yet become an integral part of most teacher education programmes. Indeed, one analysis of the international scene states that "There has been no teacher education initiative that has strategically set out to mainstream sustainability into the core of teacher education programs".[10]

The experiences of the teacher educators in the UNESCO network, mentioned above, indicate that 'this lack of progress' stems from many sources, including: a lack of vision or awareness of the role education could play in achieving sustainability at the level of schools and school curriculum and assessment boards (therefore, it is hard to justify in teacher education), a similar lack of understanding among faculty members and college/university administrators, and a perception that teacher education is an already over-crowded field with "too many disparate initiatives, too little time for thinking about new ideas, and too little encouragement to ... make links between initiatives, particularly where cultural norms or existing mission statements don't mention sustainability".[11]

Approaches to Change

In order to improve this situation, one research report has critically analysed the main types of initiatives or strategies that have been used to try to support ESD through teacher education.[12] These are: the collaborative resource development and adaptation model, the action research model and the whole-of-system model. The advantages and potential problems of each are described and illustrated by examples from around the world. Titled *Whole-school Approaches to Sustainability: A Review of Models for Professional Development in Pre-service Teacher Education*, this report is among the most comprehensive to date and makes a most worthwhile contribution. However, it has three small problems. First, it confuses issues associated with the professional development of teachers with those of teacher educators. Second, it assumes that there is one ideal way of promoting teacher education for ESD—through a whole-school (faculty? institute?) approach—and does not give sufficient recognition to other approaches. Third, it did not examine ways of addressing the factors behind the slow reorientation of teacher education for ESD.

Workshop questions

This workshop will seek to address ways in which we can

build capacity for the wider and successful implementation of ESD through initial perservice and continuing in-service teacher education. To this end, the workshop will seek answers to questions such as:

- What concepts of ESD are most relevant to school learning and teacher education?
- What contributions can teacher education make to the successful planning and teaching of ESD?
- What are the key challenges for enhancing teacher education for ESD?
- How may the range of initiatives in teacher education for ESD that have been initiated by the DESD be categorized?
- What factors have contributed to the relative degree of success of these initiatives?
- What impetus has the DESD brought to this field?
- What can be done to enhance the up-take of UNESCO guidelines on teacher education for ESD?
- What are the key priorities for the next five years of the DESD?

REFERENCES

1. See http://unesdoc.unesco.org/images/0014/00143314330 E.pdf
2. See http://www.environment.gov.au/education/publications/tsw/ index.html
3. See at http://www.ens.gu.edu.au/ciree/LSE/MAIN.HTM
4. See http://www.unesco.org/education/tlsf
5. See http://www.nepa.gov.jm/neecweb/actionplan/planbooktableof contents.htm
6. See http://seed.schule.at/
7. Seewww.ensi.org

8. See http://www.col.org/colweb/site/pid/3895
9. See http://www,unep.org/Training/features/mesa.asp
10. See http://www.aries.mq.edu.au/pdf/TeacherEduDec06.pdf (p. 10)
11. See Reference 1
12. See Reference 10

Workshop—17

Monitoring and Evaluation of ESD during the DESD

The Context

The launch of the United Nations Decade in Education for Sustainable Development (DESD) in 2005 marked the beginning of a worldwide movement which seeks to improve opportunities and quality in Education for Sustainable Development (ESD). Spanning 2005 to 2014, the DESD is a global platform looks to: *(i)* embed sustainable development into all learning spheres; *(ii)* re-orient education; and *(iii)* develop initiatives that can showcase the special role of education.

The scope of the DESD is broad and its potential effects are far reaching. If it is successful, the DESD could transform not only education but also the quality of life of many across the globe. For this reason it is important to look at ways in which we can effectively monitor progress and capture learnings in the process of implementation.

The DESD is facilitated and promoted by UNESCO which was designated as the international lead agency. It has the responsibility of establishing mechanisms for monitoring and evaluation and for reporting on progress to the UN General Assembly as well as to the UNESCO Executive Board. UNESCO established a Monitoring and Evaluation Expert Group (MEEG) to advice on appropriate monitoring mechanisms for assessing progress in ESD during the DESD years. The MEEG support the global monitoring and evaluation progress undertaken by UNESCO.

Key to the DESD, is its International Implementation Scheme (US) (2005), which sets the major thrusts of ESD as well as global milestones for the ten-year period. This document provided a basis for reporting and highlighted central role of monitoring and evaluation to the process of learning to change.

This workshop is facilitated by members of the MEEG, and supported by UNESCO DESD Secretariat, who are seeking to provide an opportunity for reflection, learning as well as skills development in the area of ESD monitoring and evaluation. The workshop organizers and facilitators recognise that monitoring and evaluation processes can assist in assessing change but also acknowledge the importance of involving stakeholders from different cultures, contexts and levels of experience in ESD in the 'learning' process which results from reflecting upon progress.

Seven key questions underpin this workshop

Q. What has been achieved in ESD during the DESD and how can this be captured?

Q. What systems and evidence exists for assessing progress in ESD?

Q. What other types/form of progress should we be trying to assess during the DESD?

Q. Where are the opportunities and the challenges for assessing progress in ESD?

Q. What mechanisms exist for involving multi-stake-holder groups in monitoring and evaluation during the DESD?

Q. How will we recognise achievement—what are we looking for?

These questions are explored through a series of participatory learning activities and workshop approach outlined below.

The Workshop

Conference Aims: As the UN DESD reaches its mid-point, the conference will highlight the essential contribution of ESD to achieving quality education, promote intercultural exchange on ESD, undertake stock-taking of DESD implementation and develop strategies for the way forward.

Workshop: Monitoring and Evaluation of ESD during the DESD-Achievements, Mechanisms and Indicators for Measuring Progress.

Date: 2nd April - 9am -1pm

Thematic Cluster: **III** Capacity development for ESD

Cluster Coordinator: Akpezi Ogbuigwe

Languages: English and French - simultaneous translation provided.

Focus

Thematic scope: This workshop will provide opportunities for participants to be actively engaged in issues associated with monitoring and evaluating of ESD during the DESD. They will be asked to engage in a scenario planning situation and fish bowl exercises as well as in group discussions and analysis. The workshop activities will: confirm the importance of M&E; contextualize the realities, issues and limitations of monitoring and evaluation of ESD given the current lack of established monitoring systems; discuss possibilities for evidence based evaluation; explore mechanisms for multi-stakeholder participation and, seek new insights and perspectives on how to improve and deveiop better data collection systems in ESD.

The interactive workshop will also provide opportunities for capacity building as various ESD indicators types are explored and group activities help develop new skills for the establishment of M&E systems.

Approach: As per Conference guidelines no formal presentations will be made. Participants will work in pairs as well as in small groups (5 per group) leading to discussions in larger groups (17/18 per group). There will be 3 resource person as well as the workshop coordinator facilitating the activities.

Key Workshop Qs

Q. What has been achieved in ESD during the DESD and how can this be captured?

Q. What systems and evidence exists for assessing progress in ESD?

Q. What other types/form of progress should we be trying to assess during the DESD?

Q. Where are the opportunities and the challenges for assessing progress in ESD?

Q. What mechanisms exist for involving multi-stake-holder groups in monitoring and evaluation during the DESD?

Q. How will we recognise achievement? What are we looking for?

Alignment with Conference Objectives

These questions as well as the approaches used in the workshop will generate discussion around all four conference objectives:

(1) ESD and its essential contribution to quality education
(2) promote international exchange on ESD
(3) carry out stock-taking of DESD implementation
(4) develop strategies for the way ahead.

Outcomes

- An appreciation of what can and cannot be monitored and assessed in ESD given existing systems and resources.
- An appreciation of the challenges faced by the UNESCO when attempting to assess progress in ESD during the Decade.
- A clearer understanding of the possibilities available for monitoring and evaluating ESD effectively.
- A clearer understanding of the variety of indicators as well as outcomes, outputs and impacts that can arise out of ESD efforts.
- Skills to be able to effectively contribute to the improvement/development of new data collection systems for M&E.

Programme

9.00 Welcome and brief introduction

9.15 Ice-breaker activity—What has been achieved in ESD during the first four years?

9.45 Small Group discussions—Process, Problems and Possibilities for M&E

10.30 Break

10.45 Fish Bowl Exercise-M&E—What are we able to assess and how?

11.15 Carousel - Indicators of Progress

12.00 Large Group discussions—Multi-stakeholder engagement and participatory evaluation approaches.

12.30 Workshop rapporteur presents main workshop outcomes to be reported by the Cluster rapporteur to the main conference. Further information about how to become involved in cycle 2 of the DESD M&E will be made available.

1.00 End

Workshop Coordination

Prof Daniella Tilbury, Chair, UN DESD Global Monitoring and Evaluation Expert Group (MEEG). Daniella is Professor of Sustainability and Director of academic and strategic development in sustainability at the University of Gloucestershire, Cheltenham Email: dtilbury@glos.ac.uk

Facilitators

Mr Roel Van Rajii, Chair of the UNECE Expert Group of ESD Indicators and member of the MEEG. He is a senior civil servant in the Dutch Ministry of Agriculture. Email: r.m.van.raaij@minlnv.nl.

Mr Pierre Varcher, Leader of the ESD Process for DESD, UNESCO Nat Com, Switzerland. Pierre is a member of MEEG. Email: pvarcher@ip-worldcom.ch.

Prof Alex Michalos, an academic specialising in matters of evaluation and national assessment. He is the Chancellor of the University of Northern British Columbia and a member of the MEEG. Email: michalos@unbc.ca.

Rapporteur

Ms *Ingrid Mula, a* Phd Student in ESD who has expertise in matters associated with monitoring and evaluation. Her role is to capture the important aspects of the discussions and outcomes of the workshop.

Relevant Background Documents

Elias, D. 2006. 'UNESCO's Approach to Implementing the Decade of Education for Sustainable Development (DESD) in Asia and the Pacific'. *Australian Journal of Environmental Education,* 22: 273-275.

Gonzalez-Gaudiano, E. 2005. The Decade of Education for Sustainable Development: Challenges and Opportunities in Mexico'. *Applied Environmental Education and Communication, 4(3):* 273-275.

Paden, M. 2007. 'Tracking Progress in the UN Decade of Education for Sustainable Development'. The *Journal of Education for Sustainable Development,* 1(1): 115-116.

Pigozzi, M. 2007. 'Quality in Education Defines ESD'. The Journal of Education for Sustainable Development, 1(1): 27-35.

Tilbury, D. (2007) *'Monitoring and Evaluation during the UN Decade of Education for Sustainable Development'*, The Journal of Education for Sustainable Development, 1(2): 239-254.

Tilbury, D., Janousek, S., Elias, D. and Bacha, J. (2007) *'Asia Pacific Guidelines for the Development of Education for Sustainable Development Indicators'* Bangkok: UNESCO Asia and Pacific Regional Bureau for Education and IUCN.

Tilbury, D., Janousek, S., Elias, D. and Bacha, J. (2007) *'Developing Indicators on Education for Sustainable Development for DESD: A quick reference guide'* Bangkok: UNESCO Asia and Pacific Regional Bureau for Education and IUCN. (Available in English and Spanish).

Tilbury, D., and Janousek, S. (2007) *'Monitoring and Assessment During the UN Decade: A summary of documented experiences on the development of ESD Indicators'*. Canberra: Australian Government Department of the Environment and Heritage and Australian Research Institute in Education for Sustainability.

UN (United Nations). 2005. United Nations General Assembly resolutions 59/237. http://daccessdds. un.org/doc/UNDOC/GEN/N04/490/48/PDF/N0449048.pdf?OpenElement.

UNECE (United Nations Economic Commission for Europe). 2005. Background paper on development of Indicators to measure implementation of the UNECE strategy for ESD. UNECE Expert Group on Indicators for Education for Sustainable Development, http:// www.unece.org/env/esd

UNESCO (United Nations Educational, Scientific and Cultural Organisation). (2005). United Nations Decade of Education for Sustainable Development (2005-2014): International Implementation Scheme. October 2005. Paris: UNESCO.

UNESCO (United Nations Educational, Scientific and Cultural Organisation). (2005). Report by the Director-General on the United Nations Decade of Education for Sustainable Development: International Implementation Scheme and UNESCO's contribution to the implementation of the Decade. August 2005. Paris: UNESCO.

UNESCO (United Nations Educational, Scientific and Cultural Organisation). (2007). The UN Decade of Education for Sustainable Development (DESD 2005-2014). The First Two Years'. Paris: UNESCO.

UNESCO (United Nations Educational, Scientific and Cultural Organisation). (2007). Education For All. Global Action Plan: Improving support to countries in achieving the EFA goals. Paris: UNESCO.

UNESCO (United Nations Educational, Scientific and Cultural Organisation). (2008) UN DESD Global Monitoring and Evaluation Framework (GMEF). Paris: UNESCO.

CHAPTER

Workshop—18

EFA-ESD Dialogue

Creating Synergies and Linkages for Educating for a Sustainable World

The objective of the workshop is to highlight the potential synergies and linkages between Education for All (EFA) and Education for Sustainable Development (ESD), which are imperative for the effective promotion and achievement of EFA and the Millennium Development Goals (MDGs). Education seeks to empower people of all ages to assume responsibility for creating and enjoying a sustainable future. It is itself a basic human right but is also a vehicle for fulfilling other human rights and freedoms which must be protected, promoted and respected. Moreover, ESD has close affinities with the human rights agenda by making connections at local, national and global levels on such issues as peace, democracy, the right to development and citizenship. Raising public awareness of these issues and linking the efforts of both initiatives and their agendas, perspectives and goals, notably with respect to programme implementation at the country level, will contribute to reducing poverty and the impact of climate change, broadening access to primary education for all and enhancing healthcare provision.

According to UNESCO's Education for Sustainable Development Policy Dialogue publication, *EFA-ESD Dialogue: Educating for a sustainable world (2008)*, the EFA and ESD constituencies both aim "to create an inspirational movement, with which a wide range of people can identify, for learning and developing with others." Separate strategies on how best to achieve this goal were developed by each constituency, with some nuances about how each defines itself and carries out its agenda. EFA is largely concerned with advocating for access to quality basic education and literacy for all learners, particularly those who are most excluded, and remains an essential element in addressing broader social challenges such as HIV and AIDS, conflicts and crises, poverty and for promoting democratic values and intercultural dialogue. ESD also places emphasis on the basic values, processes and behaviours necessary to strengthen educational capacities, address poverty reduction and build sustainable livelihoods, but reaches out not only to those most in need of education but also to those in more privileged positions in society who are often seen to have a disproportionate impact on global sustainability. This broader outreach is conducive towards generating a more widespread understanding of the importance of both universal education and engaging in sustainable practices for a common global future and towards concrete lifestyle changes and more active engagement that will have lasting benefits for all individuals and communities.

The EFA goals of lifelong learning and adult literacy can benefit from the methodology and work of Paulo Friere, a well-known educator and author who also served as an advisor to UNESCO in the late 1960s and early 70s. In his work, Fiore recognized the overlaps and linkages that exist between the EFA and ESD agendas, decades in advance of the formal adoption of their frameworks in 2000 and 2005, respectively. In particular, he noted their common commitment to quality education and endorsement of education as a human right. Similar to his work and to that of 'cultural animators' who worked with illiterate peasants and oppressed persons, the EFA and ESD agendas strive to promote human rights—predominately with respect to gender equality and the rights of marginalized populations—with the overarching aim of improving health, reducing poverty and enhancing the quality of life. In other words, liberating individuals by proposing a 'humanistic and libratory conception of education[1].'

Both the EFA and ESD agendas call on the participation of all stakeholders and constituencies, including governments, bilateral and multilateral organizations, civil society organizations (CSOs), the private sector, communities and individuals. It is also important to note that certain challenges and tensions exist between EFA and ESD, such as EFA's strong focus on basic education, ESD's broader purpose beyond education, and various social and geographical differences, which limit collaboration and integration. Moreover, although the EFA goals are closely related to the MDGs, ESD's role in the achievement of the MDGs lies largely in its ability to develop educational initiatives that bring together economic, social and environmental concerns in order to effectively ad-dress such challenges as poverty and climate change. Because ESD seeks to go "beyond education and also address the social and institutional components that inhibit sustainable development," its role is essential in the integration of both agendas.

This workshop will address the mutual ESD and EFA aim of providing quality education for all via shared understanding, joint learning and multi-disciplinary approaches to meet the developmental and environmental concerns embedded in the MDGs. Creating a strong collaboration and synergy between the two constituencies will also support and strengthen efforts to promote the types of education and learning that are needed to ensure sustainability. This workshop will also address the challenges that have thus far limited the integration of the EFA and ESD agendas, such as their differing priorities, and will draw attention to the strategies ESD has put in place to address these tensions and move towards a clearer, more fully conceptualized and integrated form of sustainable development (SD) whose foundation is quality education for all.

The benefits of strategically integrating ESD view-points into the EFA agenda will also be examined during this workshop. ESD's focus on promoting such values as peace, gender equality, and respect for human rights, the environment and cultural diversity, along with its determination to challenge established models of education, will encourage the achievement of the EFA goals in a sustainable manner. Concurrently, EFA's comparative advantage of in-depth knowledge about specific issues such as strengthening cooperation between formal, non-formal and informal education, HIV and AIDS and gender empowerment can help inform and further ESD's agenda. Moreover, EFA has an array of established connections with bilateral and multilateral partners as well as mechanisms for resource mobilization and increasing public awareness that ESD could tap into.

Policy recommendations on how best to integrate the EFA and ESD agendas will be discussed during the workshop, including the following:

- ***Create effective synergy between ESD and EFA.*** Mechanisms that promote leadership development in both constituencies can be established, with strategies that aim to unify the ESD and EFA agendas and move towards a concept of Education for Sustainable Development for All (ESDFA). It will be important for both constituencies to maintain ownership over specific issues for which they have a comparative advantage, while focussing on collaborative contributions toward achieving the MDGs and the EFA goals.

- ***Alliances must be built with bilateral, emerging/new and multilateral donors.*** Multi-dimensional approaches and new partnerships must be actively promoted at the international, regional and national levels in order to develop more comprehensive responses and holistic approaches to meet all of the internationally-agreed development goals.
- ***ESD and EFA can move toward joint monitoring and assessment.*** Establishing practices focussed on joint monitoring will allow for more thorough analyses of the approaches and programmes that are most efficiently addressing both ESD and EFA priorities. Regional events and workshops focused on joint reporting practices will help move more quickly toward a shared concept of providing quality education for all.

REFERENCE

1. Education for Social Transformations, n.a. Approach: action-research related to education and training. United Nations Educational, Scientific and Cultural Organization. Retrieved March 10, 2009.

CHAPTER

Workshop—19

Better Schools at Pre-school, Primary and Secondary Levels through ESD

Objectives

This workshop will provide participants with an opportunity to :

- explore how the concept of sustainability can transform formal education at pre-school, primary and secondary levels;
- consider in greater detail how education for sustainability can enrich and reanimate teaching/ learning strategies, the curriculum, pedagogy and the role of the teacher, and the school environment;
- share and learn from each other about how schools in different countries are responding to the call for education for sustainability.

Abstract

Education for sustainable development implies a transformation in every aspect of school life at pre-school, primary and secondary levels. At policy level, governments need to establish links between education for sustainable development and education for all, recognizing that the purpose of education is not just to support economic development, but to help individuals ahd societies develop to their fullest potential, without undermining the health of the society at large or the environment. But at the grassroots level, in schools, much can and must be done by school leaders, teachers and students to integrate sustainability into all aspects of school life and the curriculum, drawing out the interconnections between social, environmental, cultural, and economic problems and achievements. School level initiatives can respond best to the context, opportunities and needs of particular communities and the natural environment. In this workshop, participants will have the opportunity to hear, share, and critique concrete experiences, projects, and strategies from schools trying to integrate education for sustainability into their programmes. Through sharing circles and small group work tasks, participants will consider in greater detail how education for sustainability can enrich and re-animate teaching/learning strategies, the curriculum, pedagogy and the role of the teacher, and the school environment.

Concept Note

Education is fundamental for achieving sustainability and for creating a more sustainable future. All teachers can contribute to education for sustainability: mathematics can work with data that refer to pollution of environment, the poverty growth; linguistics can analyze the role played by means communication and propaganda in consumption habits; history and social sciences can discuss ethnic issues and gender inequality.

Sustainability implies a curricular reorientation, so that some principles may be incorporated to them. These principles should, for example, orientate on the conceiving of contents and elaboration of school material. Jean Piaget has taught us that a curriculum should include things that are meaningful to students. We know, this is correct, but incomplete. The contents that are present in the curriculum have to be meaningful to the student, and they will only be meaningful to them, if these contents are also meaningful to the health of the planet.

Regarding the impact of the concept of sustainability at the formal education, we can considers two levels: *(a)* The legal level: educational reforms (curriculum, contents). The law, the rule, can introduce new behaviours, but, we need an other level; *(b)* The level of the commitment of persons, engaging her/his endorsement (for a sustainable lifestyle), by a virotic process, biological, intuitive (not mechanic or rational process), possible by different motivations (compassion, love, fear, anger, etc.).

ESD is a integrative (integrate education, health, jobs, sciences, etc.) and interactive concept. We need, for example, to establish a dialog between ESD and Education For All (EFA) strategies. EFA have made a long way (Jomtien, Dakar...). ESD is beginning. We need to create synergies between this two processes and use the concept of sustainability to implement a new quality of formal education, a socio-environmental education. In this moment, the rich countries have more attention to ESD and the poor countries, due to his reality, have more attention to EFA.

What is the different of emphasis between this tow movements? EFA refers to basic education, formal system, to basic learning needs, to schools, literacy, to the right of education. Basically, EFA involve just the Ministry of Education. By contrary, ESD movement go beyond the basic education and formal education. He is also non-formal, and involve the lifelong learning education (social level, systems and organizations). However, ESD, serve to reorient curricula. It is more emancipatory and involve other Ministries, like Environment, Agriculture, etc.

We need to re-orientate existent educational programme in the sense of promoting knowledge, competences and abilities, principles, values and attitudes related to sustainability. A concrete strategy so that we can start this debate inside our schools and building an eco-audit in order to discover where exactly we are being unsustainable. It is very simple: we only need to trace everything we do and compare this data to the principles of sustainability. It is not hard to identify where we are and where we are not integrating in our curriculum, in a broad sense, the concepts of sustainable development, in history, in social sciences and in our daily lives.

In terms of level of teaching, we have to adopt different strategies: in primary school, for example, our children need to experience (experiences stick more than talking) and they need to know the plants' and animals' needs, their habitat, how to reduce, re-use and recycle materials that have been used, how to keep ecosystems attached to forests and water. In a more advanced level, we need to discuss biodiversity, environmental conservation, alternatives of energy and global warming. At university level, besides diffusing environmental information, we need to produce new knowledge and do research that aim at looking for a new development paradigm.

Among the pedagogical values and principles of a eco-pedagogy, we can highlight: educate for a global thinking; educate one's feelings; teach our identity in the Earth as a vital human condition; educate for planetary awareness; educate for understanding and educate for voluntary simplicity and quietness.

Essentially, the Decade of Education For Sustainable Development aims at making people aware through means of their disposal. Therefore, it will work with ethical values and principles which are related to people's sustainable life and to the planet's survival itself. For this reason, the Decade is, above all, a call for a transforming action, a call for popular education, for an education for and to planetary citizenship, for an instertranscultural and intertransdisciplinaty dialogue, for a culture of peace and sustainability that promotes the end of poverty, of illiteracy in the world, of political domination and economical exploitation, finally, an education for emancipation.

Educate for sustainability is educate for another possible world, educate to living in the cosmos—cosmo-logical education—broadening our comprehension of Earth and universe. It is educate for having a cosmic perspective. This is the only way we will be able to understand better problems like desertification, deforestation, global warming etc. Classical paradigms, arrogantly anthropocentric and industry-oriented, do not have enough reach to explain this cosmic reality. Since they do not have this holistic view, they were not able to give answers in the sense of how to take the world off of this route that leads to extermination and to cruel differences between the rich and the poor. Classical paradigms are leading the planet to a loss of natural resources. The current crisis regards civilizatory paradigms. Educate for sustainability needs a new paradigm, a holistic one.

What can schools do in order to save the planet? The EDS's main goal is to influence on curricular change by introducing the theme sustainability. Some countries have already started. In order to promote this chance. Implementing the concept of sustainability in school curricula, make them more flexible, involving teachers, students, parents and communities, associating formal and non-formal education. The community, in and out of the school, meets in order to discuss the theme and to build eco-political-pedagogical projects in schools, attaching education and sustainability. The result is the construction of a eco-school.

ESD needs to have a school approach, like the Eco-School concept developed in many countries. Apart from building environmental awareness, and positive environmental attitudes and values, it also needs to be reflected in the day to day running of the school, in the non-formal curriculum or hidden curriculum. We cannot teach students about energy conservation in their science class, if the schools are not doing anything to reduce energy consumption as school level. Environmental awareness is necessary, but not enough.

A curriculum which promotes ESD must continuously be reviewed to address new environmental, social and economical crisis and see how it can be tackled at local level and perhaps, how the schools can adapt to all these changes taking place. Issues like climate change, sustainable consumption, human rights, living values and food security also need to be integrated in both the formal curriculum as well as the non-formal curriculum. Schools need to identify local problematic issues and see how it can be dealt with in their local context, through school based programme.

It must also involve the school population, not only the students, but also school managers, the teaching and non-teaching staff, the organizations and community groups which work with the school. But most importantly, ESD needs to get the support of authorities concerned; especially the Ministry of Education to ensure that is in cooperated in the school formal educational system.

In summary, ESD is a great opportunity to renew the curricula of formal educational systems and to promote the emergency of complex methodological epistemological approaches that may empower the inter-disciplinary and the inter-transculturality. EDS is a great opportunity to the teachers at all levels, to schools and university heads, to students, education ministers and other education politicians, to change all levels of our education systems.

Workshop—20

The Role of Higher Education and Research in ESD

Introduction

Higher education and research have much to contribute to the global effort for education for sustainable development (ESD). The vast majority of today's leaders attended institutions of higher education (IHEs) and the leaders of tomorrow will also. IHEs educate or 'train' many of the professionals in our societies. Because these professionals work in or manage people who work in every economic sector both private and public, it is important that higher education incorporate sustainability into all of its programmes.

IHEs are traditionally thought of as being active in three realms: teaching, research, and outreach/community service. The balance of these three depends on the institution. Some institutions are primarily teaching institutions while other also incorporate large portions of research. Some specialize in bridging theory with practice, giving students the opportunity to apply their learning in the surrounding communities. Regardless of the emphasis within the three, the United

Nations Decade of Education for Sustainable Development (UNDESD) calls IHEs to envision and incorporate sustainability into the programmes, practices, and policies of each institution.

Challenges to IHEs and research institutions related to ESD include providing professional development opportunities for administrators and staff so they can become aware of and have respect for the value of incorporating sustainability into the activities of the IHE. Faculty members also need professional development to describe their course content, research, and service in terms of sustainability. The next challenge is to incorporate and implement sustainability in all institutional activities. It is not enough to weave sustainability into current coursework or create additional courses related to sustainability. IHEs must also incorporate sustainability into all of their activities, buildings, policies, etc. so that the institution models sustainability in addition to teaching sustainability.

Access to and Retention in Quality Higher Education

The first thrust of ESD for the UNDESD is access and retention in quality basic education. Although higher education is not technically basic education, higher education is foundational to the creation of sustainable societies. The issue of access to higher education is pervasive around the world. Can students, who merit entrance on an academic basis, gain equal access to higher education regardless of social class and ethnicity? Unfortunately, economic, social, and geographic barriers prevent enrollment. The same barriers also lower student retention in IHEs. Without additional support underprivileged students too often do not complete their degree programs. Sustainability is so important to all geographic regions, social classes, and ethnic groups within our respective nations that we need to strive to assure equity in access to and retention in higher education. Only through such equity can the next generation of leadership understand and implement sustainability across our nations.

The first thrust of ESD emphasizes quality. Defining quality education for primary, secondary, or higher education is difficult. In the new millennium, however, one key characteristic of quality in higher education is sustainability is part of the curriculum.

Reorienting Higher Education to Address Sustainability

Reorienting existing education to address sustainability is another of the four thrusts of the UNDESD. What does it mean to reorient education to address sustainability? It means incorporating more knowledge, skills, issues, values, and perspectives related to sustainability into existing coursework and programmes. Several disciplines and professions have taken the lead in defining what should be taught within their fields to address sustainability. For example, engineers in Australia and teacher educators around the globe have created recommendations for reorienting education provided through IHEs.

IHEs around the world are challenged to answer "what to teach" related to sustainability. It is easy to generate a long list of environmental, social, and economic concepts, paradigms, facts, issues, ideologies, theories, conceptual frameworks, etc. related to sustainability. Such a list rapidly grows cumbersome—too long to teach. IHEs and other organizations are attempting to identify 'core competencies' or understandings that every student should have when they graduate. However, the list of such competencies is also long given the complexity of sustainability. In addition, given that all ESD must be locally relevant and culturally appropriate a list must be created to address the environmental, social and economic contexts of each IHE.

Another effort to define what students should know, do and value when they graduate is to identify learning outcomes. Many IHEs seek to find answers to core questions about what really matters in college or university. Portland State

University has worked for 18 months on identifying campus-wide learning outcomes, which will be implemented by the various academic departments on campus to reflect disciplinary differences. PSD learning outcomes include: creative and critical thinking, communication, diversity, ethics and social responsibility, internationalization, engagement, and sustainability. All of these contribute to ESD.

Addressing Sustainability beyond the Classroom

IHEs also have unique opportunities to model sustainability throughout their campuses by changing practices and policies. Some large IHEs are like miniature cities providing housing, food services, employment, transportation, utilities, entertainment, shopping, etc. to the thousands of people who visit campus each day. IHEs can demonstrate sustainability through purchasing practices, green construction and renovation, water and energy conservation, equitable hiring practices by gender and ethnicity, payment of a livable wage, etc. In this way the human-built environment and the human and economic interactions all reflect sustainability. IHEs can be leaders in communities where perhaps few other sustainable practices are evident. In this way students become accustomed to seeing sustainability and will carry those expectations with them to their future places of employment.

Research to Support ESD

Research Institutions and IHEs can do much to support ESD for the remainder of the DESD. The UNESCO Roadmap for Creating a Research Founda-tion to Support the UNDESD identifies research as a means to advance progress in ESD. A need exists for:

- Analysis of policy (e.g., which educational policies promote or thwart ESD);
- Analysis of curriculum (e.g., identify current threads of sustainability in the curriculum and make recommendations for filling the gaps);

- Evaluation of practices (e.g., identify good practices and develop case studies);

  A need also exists for other avenues of research including:

- Measurement of increasing competencies related to sustainability;
- Documenting the extent of changes in IHEs related to ESD.

Many IHEs carry out research that if guided appropriately could greatly enhance ESD in IHEs and other educational settings.

Objectives of the Workshop

1. To learn the current status of ESD in IHEs around the world.
2. To analyze current activities in IHEs related to ESD and distill lessons learned.
3. To create a vision for IHEs related to ESD
4. To identify next steps to help create the vision in the remainder of the UNDESD.

Questions to Guide the Discussion

1. What are the current successes and challenges for IHEs to weave sustainability into the course work (e.g., assessing learning outcomes and defining core competencies), research, and outreach as well as using sustainability to guide institutional practices (e.g., gender and ethnic equity in hiring) and policies (e.g., retrofitting buildings for energy conservation).
2. What are the lessons learned from the activities related to ESD, which we have heard about so far in this session?

3. What support (e.g., financial and other resources, a supportive legislative framework, enlightened policy at ministry level, opportunities for professional development) is needed beyond institutions of higher education to support efforts within IHEs to integrate sustainability into the curriculum, programmes, practices, and policies of campuses?
4. Let's create a vision of an ideal IHE in terms of ESD.
5. What are the next steps for making progress toward this vision for IHEs during the second half of the UNDESD?

REFERENCES

1. UNESCO (2005) *United Nations Decade of Education for Sustainable Development: Draft International Implementation Scheme 2005-2015*, Paris: UNESCO.
2. UNESCO. (2007). Roadmap for Creating a Research Foundation to Support the UNDESD. Paris: UNESCO.

CHAPTER

Workshop—21

Education for Sustainable Development and Life-long Learning

Globalisation should... lead to the promotion of shared understanding, values and cooperative actions on a transnational and trans-societal level. It would be a movement that recognizes and respects the diversity, variety and richness of local discourses, codes and practices, while developing viewpoints and the understanding that facilitates cooperation and coordination at a global and totally inclusive level.

(Catherine Odora, 2003, p. 14)

Learning for sustainable development is a process that continues life long and therefore takes place in a whole range of learning environments that may be formal, non-formal and informal in nature; the ultimate objective is 'a better future for all'.

(Heideveld & Cornelissen, 2008, p. 15)

One of the challenges of lifelong learning for sustainable development is how to put global solidarity, rather than international competitiveness at the heart of learning. ***(Scandrett, 2008, p. 7)***

Introduction

There have been a number of recent initiatives designed to foster dialogue between those working in the fields of lifelong learning and education for sustainable development (ESD). These include a South-South policy forum on lifelong learning, held in Jakarta (UIL, 2008), that produced a strategy paper calling for a clear conceptualization of lifelong learning and vision of sustainable development; essential competences for social, cultural, environmental and economic development; learning strategies conducive to sustainable development; and institutional mechanisms to support lifelong learning for sustainable development (LLLSD). In June 2008 the national commission for Unesco in the Netherlands held a conference that recognized two priorities: establishing North/South dialogue, and clarifying terminology.

This workshop has been planned to reflect the strategies and priorities established at those conferences. We recognize that the theory and practice of the related fields of sustainable development, lifelong learning and ESD is diverse and contested and that it is unrealistic to expect agreement on those concepts, visions, competences, learning strategies, and institutional support mechanisms that should guide LLLSD. Any attempt to survey the constituent fields of LLLSD in this background paper would be counter productive as it might shape or limit the views expressed in the workshop. Instead we have used this paper to outline the objectives, activities, and key questions of a workshop that should enable diverse theory and practice to be shared, celebrated in a future collection of case studies, and serve as a pointer to necessary institutional reforms.

What follows outlines the five stages of the workshop and associates each with one or more of the objectives, key questions and outcomes listed in the table on page two. Like all workshop outlines this one is provisional. What happens on the day partly depends on your responses.

Activity—1: Meeting Other Practitioners (*Objective 1, Key question 1*)

First we will do an activity to give everyone an understanding of who is represented/not represented in the whole group.

Objectives	Key Questions	Outcomes
1	2	3
1. Appreciate and understand the diversity of approaches to lifelong learning for sustainable development (LLLSD) practiced in different contexts around the world.	1. How is LLLSD best conceptualised and what *principles* should inform its practice? Are there ways to differentiate along cultural or North-South lines? Is there a coherent approach at the national level?	1. *A systematic synopsis* of the different positions and ways to differentiate them.
2. Reflect on different meanings of lifelong learning and sustainable development and thereby better understand the range of theoretical and political principles underpinning LLLSD.	2. How should LLLSD engage with *people's existing knowledge, skills, ways of viewing the world, and learning agendas?* How should it equip them to recognize and potentially transcend social norms, group thinking and personal biases? What *competences (knowledge, skills and values)* will they need to cope with new natural, social, political and economic conditions, and to give shape and meaning to their lives?	2. *A wall display* that illustrates the participants' understandings of sustainable development, life-long learning, and LLSD.
3. Evaluate two gase studies of LLLSD in terms of their potential to draw on local knowledge and contribute to the alleviation of	3. What *learning strategies may* enable people to become more sensitive to and learn from alternative ways of knowing,	3. *A briefing document* that will allow participants to submit *case studies* of LLLSD to a standard format following the workshop.

(Contd...)

1	2	3
poverty and the improvement of social, economic and educational outcomes for disadvantaged groups.	valuing and doing? How can LLLSD close theory/practice (values/action) gaps and develop new forms of *(environmental, ecological, global) citizenship?*	Short case studies are likely to focus on the princi-ples of LLLSD guiding practice, the inputs provided by local people, the knowledge, skills and competences developed, and the learning strategies employed.
4. Explain institutional changes that may be necessary to increase the connections between formal, informal and non-formal ESD and to shift the policy agenda from basic education for all to basic ESD for all.	4. How should we create *formal, non-formal and informal settings* that are conducive to the emergence of LLLSD and what *institutional changes* would enable basic ESD for all? (with acknowledgement to Wals (ed.), 2007, p. 19)	4. *Recommendations* regarding those institutional issues that would increase the connections between formal, informal and non-formal ESD; and to shift the policy agenda from basic education for all to basic ESD for all,
		5. *The posters* will be displayed on the wall for you to compare and then Antoine Heideveld from the Netherlands will reflect upon them the different interests and perspectives in the light of his research on LLLSD. He will provide a systematic synopsis of the different positions and ways to differentiate them.

Then in twos, you will introduce yourself to a person you have not met before. Then you will both share your knowledge of each other with another pair of participants. In this way you will get to know a little more about three people, their backgrounds, and why they are at the workshop.

Activity—2: Analyzing and Discussing Statements about LLSD *(Objective 2, Key question 1 and 2, Outcome 1 and 2)*

This activity is planned in a way to deepen and systematize further the different positions and approaches with regard to LLLESD. You will be given an activity sheet on which there are five short statements about those competences (knowledge, skills and values) that LLLSD should develop (see below). You will be invited to write your own sixth statement that better reflects your own conceptualization of LLLSD. The aim of Activity one is to highlight the different perspectives and interests in the field of LLLSD.

Five statements about Lifelong Learning for Sustainable Development

A. LLLSD should develop those competences that people require to develop appropriate technologies and sustainable livelihoods within the informal economy.

B. LLLSD should develop those competencies that would improve the labour market for environmentally friendly technologies, and thus LLLSDs relevance for employment.

C. LLLSD should not develop pre-determined competences. Those that people require will only emerge as they address issues facing their community and learn alongside others.

D. LLLSD should develop those competences that people require to resist the further dispossession and privatisation of environmental knowledge and resources and work with others to realize environmental justice.

(Contd...)

> ***E. LLLSD should develop those competences that people require to understand their relations with one another and the rest of nature and realise forms of citizenship that enable the continued co-evolution of human and non-human nature.***

Next you will be asked to discuss in groups the statements you have been given and those you have written. Who is likely to support each statement and what conceptualizations of sustainable development and lifelong learning do they reflect? In what ways are any two or more of the statements complementary or contradictory?

Then your group will be asked to select one of the statements. It may be the one that claims most support from group members or the one about which group members show most interest. You will write this statement at the top of a poster and below it list the principles (beliefs and values) that, in the group's opinion, inform it. Also on this poster you will list no more than four key texts or articles that have enabled group members to increase their understanding of different conceptualisations of education and lifelong learning for sustainable development.

Activity—3: Case Studies of LLLSD *(Objective 3, Key question 1 and 2, Outcome 3)*

The focus will shift to key question 2 and the ways in which this is answered by practitioners working in varied contexts across the world. Lui Yunhua from China, and Muhammad Ibrahim from Bangladesh will present case studies of current practice and you will have an opportunity to ask questions.

Your attention will then be drawn to outcome 2 and UNESCO's intention of publishing a collection of such case studies. Working in small groups you will write the outline of a briefing paper to guide the authors of these studies. A number of groups will report back explaining the outline they propose before the processes whereby the actual briefing is prepared, case studies submitted, and the publication compiled and edited, are discussed.

Activity—4: Making Recommendations about Institutional Changes to Enable LLLSD (*Objective 4, Key question 4, Outcome 4*)

Ms Koumba Bolly Barry from Burkina Faso will address key question 4 by outlining those institutional changes in her country that would in her view encourage greater synergy: between formal and informal BSD; and shift the policy agenda towards basic ESD for all. She will be followed by two or three participants who would also outline institutional changes in her/his country. The aim is to highlight the different ways to solve the problems with regard to interrelationships between formal, non-formal and informal ESD.

You will then be asked to recommend the two institutional changes that, in your view, would best enable these goals to be realized in your own country. These recommendations will be taken to a conference in Brazil (Adult Education for viable and sustainable futures) in May 2009

We look forward to meeting you in Bonn.

Please bring a copy of this paper to the workshop.

Mr Adama Ouane and Ms Madhu Singh UNESCO Institute of Lifelong Learning www.unesco.org/uil

Ms Liu Yunhua and Mr John Huckle

Shangri-La Institute for Sustainable Communities

www.shangrilainstitute.org

http://john.huckle.org.uk

Workshop coordinators and facilitators

REFERENCES

1. Indigenous Knowledge and the Integration of Knowledge Systems, C. A. Odura (ed.), 2003,
2. Learning for Sustainable Development, Exploring Learning Strategies Across the Lifespan, A. Heideveld & S. Cornelissen, Cinop/Unesco, 2008
3. Lifelong Learning for Ecological Sustainability and Environmental Justice, E. Scandrett, 2008 (http://www.niace.org.uk/lifelonglearninginquiry/ docs/Eurig-Scandrett-ecological-sustainability.pdf)
4. Strategy paper resulting from South-South Policy Forum on Lifelong Learning as the key to Sustainable Development help in Jakarta, UIL, 2008 Learning for Sustainability (http://learningfor sustainability.net/)
5. Social Learning, Towards a Sustainable World, A. Wals (ed.), Wageningen Academic Publishers, 2007.

CHAPTER

Workshop—22

Developing Skills and Labour Force Competencies including TVET in Support of Sustainable Development

TVET and A 'New Development Paradigm'

1. Moving towards the goal of sustainable development requires fundamental changes in human attitudes and behaviour—in our personal lives, in our community activities, and in our places of work. Successfully making these changes is critically dependent on education and training. This is no more important than in the area of developing skills for employability, citizenship and sustainability in the world of work.
2. Thus, the Second International Conference on Technical and Vocational Education (TVET) (Seoul, 1999) concluded that a new paradigm of both development and of preparation for the world of work was needed:

   We have considered the emerging challenges of the twenty-first century, a century that will be an era of knowledge, information and communication. Globalization and the revolution in information and communication technology have signalled the need for a new human-centred development paradigm. We have concluded that Technical and Vocational Education (TVE), as an integral component of lifelong learning, has a crucial role to play in this new era as an effective too! to realize the objectives of a culture of peace, environmentally sound sustainable development, social cohesion, and international citizenship.[1]

3. This 'new human centred development paradigm' was elaborated through the Millennium Development Goals (MDGs).[2] Achieving the MDGs necessitates action on issues such as poverty, hunger, education, gender equality, child and maternal mortality, HIV/AIDS, safe water, upgrading slums, and global partnerships for development that include technology transfer. Effective TVET is integral to finding and implementing solutions to all of these issues. In this way, TVET underpins all the MDGs and the achievement of sustainable development.

4. Thus, a broadening of TVET from the narrow task of providing training for industry- and occupation-specific skills to the broader task of workforce development and lifelong learning for sustainable development and citizenship is currently underway. For example, the international Education for All programme emphasises vocational preparation within a context of social and environmental responsibility. Similarly, the Final Report of the 2002 World Summit on Sustainable Development emphasised the need for all countries and international agencies to meet "capacity needs for training, technical know-how and strengthening national institutions in ... economically viable, socially acceptable and environmentally sound" development in order to eradicate poverty, improve human health and access to safe water and hygienic sanitation, conserve the natural resource base upon which social and economic development depends, and

foster the use of technologies for foster cleaner production and renewable energy.[3] As a result, one of the objectives listed for TVET in the joint 2002 ILO and UNESCO *Recommendations on Technical and Vocational Education for the Twenty-First Century* is to "Empower people to contribute to environmentally sound sustainable development through their occupations and other areas of their lives."[4] This is particularly important as many people are increasingly looking for work that they consider to be personally fulfilling and socially worthwhile. Such are often to be found in the field of environment friendly technologies and the companies that promote and service them.

UNESCO's Contribution

5. One of key aims of the UNESCO-UNEVOC Centre in Bonn is to ensure that TVET systems and institutions, their staff, and the businesses with which they engage, are aware of the important contributions that TVET can make to advancing sustainable development. This has included convening seven international and regional workshops: Bonn (2004), Bangkok (2005, 2006), Bahrain (2005), Ho Chi Minh City (2006), Ahmedabad (2007) and Melbourne (2008). UNESCO-UNEVOC has also:
   - established a TVET and Sustainable Development section on the UNESCO-UNEVOC website;
   - published detailed reports of these meetings on this website, including all presentations;
   - initiated an e-Forum titled "Two pathways, one destination TVET for a sustainable future" that attracted 106 participants from 49 countries;
   - sponsored the Asia Pacific Network for International and Values Education to develop a curriculum on ESD and TVET, titled *Learning to Do;*

- sponsored joint projects between UNEVOC Centres to address the issues of ESD and TVET (e.g. between Griffith University and Zhejiang Technology Institute of Economy UNEVOC Centres);
- conducted two high level meetings with the corporate sector to identify ways in which the business and industry can integrate education, training and capacity building for sustainable development into its CSR programme; and
- sponsored theoretical rethink on the role of TVET and sustainable development as well as a publication of a 36-chapter book of case studies on initiatives around the world to reorient TVET for Sustainable Development.[6]

6. UNESCO-UNEVOC along with BiBB, InWEnt, CPSC and other national and international partners have also sought to align TVET with other sectors of education, seeking synergies and partnerships with secondary education and universities, seeking to enhance pathways for the school-to-work transition in order to embed sustainability in all areas of learning for the world of work.[6]

Global Partnerships and Achievements

7. International support programmes and other initiatives may be noted in many parts of the world—at the levels of national policy, in TVET systems, in individual schools, in TVET institutes and in companies.
8. Several national initiatives have worked with the concept of 'competencies'. These include for example: research to identify sustainability competencies for the world of work in Canada; establishing a framework for including sustainability competencies in Industry Training Packages in Australia; and a rethinking of the

very concept of 'competencies' and ESD in South Africa, based upon three kinds of competencies—practical, foundational and reflexive—to be integrated into all TVET programmes. In Azerbaijan, the concepts of'decent work' and 'sustainable livelihoods' are being applied to the informal economy as a to up-skill workers for jobs in the expanding oil and gas industry. A national programme called 'Learn-ing to Last' has been undertaken in the UK and a range of grant and support projects established to encourage TVET institutes to review their curricula and their campus operations. Germany has been very active in this area also and has initiated a national policy process and performed a pilot programme on ESD through BiBB.

9. There have been many exciting initiatives in individual schools and TVET institutes. For example, in countries as diverse as Colombia, Japan, Kenya and Australia many have established school-based enterprises that focus on designing, making and selling sustainable products. In China, one TVET Institute is re-skilling migrant workers displaced by major dam construction. Many are also exploring ways in which they can respond to the opportunities and challenges of climate change by rethinking the content of training programmes, especially in the construction and environmental auditing industries.

10. The corporate sector is increasingly becoming engaged in using education, training and capacity building as strategies in their CSR and sustainable development activities. This includes at least four types of activities: training for employees on corporate sustainability goals, training for employees of firms along supply chains to ensure they have the capacity to achieve corporate sustainability goals, ESD programmes for the communities that form the constituencies for different firms, and corporate support for ESD in schools, TVET colleges and universities.

Workshop Questions

11. Unfortunately, these many examples of initiatives to reorient TVET for ESD are not widespread at a global scale. They remain 'lighthouse' activities that need to be scaled up and, where appropriate adapted for local implementation, and made part of mainstream practice in TVET.

12. Ways of achieving this goal is the focus of TVET and Sustainable Development workshop. A highly interactive process will be used to explore the following questions:

    - What is the role of TVET in supporting Sustainable Development?
    - What are the opportunities and responsibilities of Member States, businesses, associations, educational institutions and civic society organisations in supporting the reorientation of TVET for Sustainable Development?
    - What role can UNESCO with national and international partners play in supporting the reorientation of TVET for Sustainable Development?
    - What lessons of leading practice can be distilled from the analysis of shared experiences?
    - What are the priorities for further advancing TVET for Sustainable Development over the next five years of the DESD?

REFERENCES

1. UNESCO (1999! *Final Report, Second International Conference on Technical and Vocational Education,* UNESCO, Paris, p. 61.
2. See http://www.un.org/millenniumgoals/.
3. World Summit on Sustainable Development (2002) *Plan of Implementation,* Johannesburg, para. 19.

4. UNESCO and ILO (2002) Technical and Vocational Education for the Twenty-First Century: ILO and UNESCO Rscommendations, UNESCO, Paris and ILO, Geneva, p. 9.

5. Pavlova, M. (2009) *Technology and Vocational Education for Sustainable Development Empowering Individuals for the Future.* Dordrecht: Springer; and Fien, J., Maclean, R. and M-G Park (2008) *Work, Learning and Sustainable Development: Opportunities and Challenges,* Springer. Dortrecht.

6. For details of the examples mentioned in this section, see various chapters in *Work, Learning and Sustainable Development: Opportunities and Challenges.*

PART—III

PROJECT-BASED WORKSHOPS

CHAPTER

Project-based Workshop—1

Water as a Source of Life (From Traditional Excursions to Streams towards Innovative Stewardship of Streams by Schools)

Short Description

This Project-based Workshop will focus on projects with the aim of increasing knowledge on water as a source of life. Participants will be divided into smaller groups and rotate between three stations. The Erich Klausener Gymnasium will present its active role within a stewardship of streams which has been in operation for more than ten years: aquatic, solid and cultural-historical problems are thematised within the classroom and through field work. As a second station, the Nature and Biodiversity Conservation Union will offer active experiences with water through the participation in experiments and practices as well as the introduction of methods related to real-life activities. The NEPTUN (new partnership for transnational understanding and co-operation in water management) project will showcase as a third station its contribution to the further development of professionals in the water management field, via development of concepts, curricula and learning content based on the European Water Framework Directive.

Workshop Schedule

1630	Arrival and welcome
1645	Introduction: Why is water a theme for education?
1700	Split-up into learning stations with the game 'Bamboleo'
1715	Parallel learning stations with hands-on activities: 1. early childhood 2. school education 3. higher education Participants have the possibility to rotate between stations every 30 minutes
1815	Summary and reflection of learning stations
1830	Plenary discussion on water as a theme for ESD
1900	Informal get-together and dinner
2000	Bus transfer to Bonn main station

More information on projects involved

http://www.nabu-wiesloch.de, http://ekgadenau3.bildung-rp.de
http://www.neptun-project.org

CHAPTER

Project-based Workshop—2

Water Quality and Research—The Ship 'MS Burgund' as a Swimming Classroom

Short Description

This Project-based Workshop will be conducted by the Ministry for Environment, Forest and Consumer Protection of the Federal State of Rhineland-Palatinate. It takes place on the research ship 'MS Burgund' on the river Rhine. Workshop participants will take part in hands-on experiences normally conducted with school classes. Stations of learning with their exercises and working material specially created as a concept of teaching and learning within secondary schools will be presented to the workshop participants. These stations are guided by authentic experts like the ship's captain and the operator of the ship who normally present the stations to students. The Project-based Workshop wants to educate participants towards being 'laboratory assistants' 'stream researchers', 'discoverers of the Rhine' and 'ship's masters'.

Workshop Schedule

1615	Arrival and take-off of the ship, welcome and safety references
1630	Observation of a sample drawing of sediment
1700	Split-up into working groups
1715	Interactive work at rotating stations: 1. laboratory 2. dissection area 3. ship deck 4. ship bridge Participants have the possibility to rotate between stations every 30 minutes
1830	Discussion on methods used, summary
1900	Informal get-together and dinner on board
2000	Guided tour to tram station

More information on projects involved

http://www.mufv.rlp.de

CHAPTER

Project-based Workshop—3

Biodiversity and Education for Sustainable Development

Short Description

This Project-based Workshop is offered by the German Federal Agency for Nature Conservation (BfN), the Bonn University Botanical Gardens and InWent Capacity Building International. The aim is to come into contact with colleagues of different countries and different backgrounds and talk about biological diversity as a key theme for ESD. Biological diversity in this context encompasses the conservation of species and habitats as well as a sustainable use. The great potential of Botanic Gardens and similar institutions for ESD in this context will be shown. On stations in the Botanic Gardens, small groups will discuss with project representatives about experiences in their own countries and opportunities for cooperation.

Workshop Schedule

1615	Arrival and welcome by W. Lobin, Botanical Gardens;
1645	C. Schnell, Federal Agency for Nature Conservation and K. Salau, InWent Split-up into learning stations
1700	Parallel learning stations with discussion groups: 1. What does biological diversity mean in the context of ESD? 2. What role does biological diversity play in educational work? 3. How can biological diversity and Education for Sustainable Development be implemented in Botanical Gardens, Zoos and similar institutions? Participants have the possibility to rotate between stations every 30 minutes
1830	Summary and conclusion
1900	Informal get-together and dinner with project presentations
2000	Bus transfer to Bonn main station

More information on projects involved

http://www.botgart.uni-bonn.de;
http://www.bfn.de;
http://www.inwent.org;
http://www.umweltstation-reichelshof.de

CHAPTER

Project-based Workshop—4

Learning Sustainability in Forests and Nature—Examples of Good Practice in Germany

Short Description

Forests are an ideal place to demonstrate the principles of sustainability: Here, nature inspires one with regard to a great variation of topics. The core of forest and nature education is to foster an understanding with all senses, based on Pestalozzi's idea of learning with 'head, heart and hands'. Forest education combines more than one educational method and has the potential to teach essential competences for a sustainable development. Moreover, the principle of sustainability will be shown through examples of forest use, e.g. forestry and hunting. In innovative projects, sustainability is a process of negotiating ecological, economic, social and cultural factors. In the Project-based Workshop, four projects of interdisciplinary teaching outside of schools in and about forests will be presented.

Workshop Schedule

1640	Arrival and welcome
1700	Short presentation 'Nature education in the forest' and overview of the different projects
1715	Split-up into working groups, interactive work on the themes: 1. Tour 'not just straight through the forest' (Querwaldein) 2. Forest meets school 3. Learning nature suitcase 4. Multipliers training and teaching modules
1830	Summary and joint discussion
1900	Informal get-together and dinner at Restaurant Waldau
2000	Bus transfer to Bonn main station

More information on projects involved

http://www.querwaldein.de
http://www.lernort-natur.de
http://portal.uni-freiburg.de/ifp
http://www.wald-mv.de

Project-based Workshop—5

From Research to Action *Implementing ESD in Higher Education*

Short Description

Due to the summer school hosted by the German Academic Exchange Service (DAAD), 50 experts from different developing countries will get together in order to address the question as to how universities can actively face up to the challenges associated with ESD, and to what extent targeted structural changes can contribute to transforming universities for sustainability. In order to address varied experiences, as well as to emphasize cultural and regional issues, two topics will be presented, namely: "Sustainable Development as Strategy and Aim of Higher Education" (University of Lüneburg) and "From Research to Practice: The Role of Education for Sustainable Development in Natural Resource Management in Research, Education and International Cooperation" (University of Greifswald). Cross-border education and cross-cultural experiences will be interactively discussed with the audience and the conference delegates. In cooperation with the United Nations University (UNU) this

Project-based Workshop fosters a diverse platform in order to empower international experts on this agenda. With this instrument, the DAAD summer school on ESD, aims to encourage an interdisciplinary and holistic approach in the field of ESD.

Workshop Schedule

1620	Arrival and welcome
1630	Panel discussion: From research to action • DAAD-Alumni from the University of Greifswald • DAAD-Alumni from the University of Luneburg • A. Ogbuigwe, Head, Environmental Education and Training, UNEP United Nations Environment Programme Nairobi • Prof. Dr. J. Pretzsch, Head of the Department of Forest Sciences, Technical University Dresden Chair: J. Bogardi, Rector of the Institute for Environment and Human Security (UNU-EHS)
1800	Interactive panel discussion and conclusions
1900	Informal get-together and dinner
2000	Bus transfer to Bonn main station

More information on projects involved

http://www.daad.de

CHAPTER

Project-based Workshop—6

ESD and the Socio-economic Dimensions *A Challenge towards Changing Behaviours and Consumption Patterns*

Short Description

Due to the summer school hosted by the German Academic Exchange Service (DAAD), 50 experts from different developing countries will get together in order to address the question as to how universities can actively face up to the challenges associated with ESD, and to what extent targeted structural changes can contribute to transforming universities for sustainability. In order to address varied experiences, as well as to emphasize cultural and regional issues, two topics will be presented, namely: "Poverty and Social Inequality in Education and its Impact on Sustainable Development" (University of Kassel) and "Sustainability within the organic chemistry lab course" (University of Braunschweig). Cross-border education and cross-cultural experiences will be interactively discussed with the audience and the conference delegates. This workshop fosters a diverse platform in order to empower international experts on this agenda. With this instrument, the DAAD summer school on ESD, aims to encourage an interdisciplinary and holistic approach in the field of ESD.

Workshop Schedule

1620	Arrival and welcome
1630	Panel discussion: From research to action • DAAD-Alumni from the University of Braunschweig • DAAD-Alumni from the University of Kassel • C. Lindberg, Member of the UNESCO High-level Panel on Education for Sustainable Development • Prof. Dr. G. Müller-Christ, Speaker of the Research Centre for Sustainability Studies University of Bremen Chair: Prof. Dr. Stefan Hormuth, President of the German Academic Exchange Service (DAAD)
1800	Interactive panel discussion and conclusions
1900	Informal get-together and dinner
2000	Bus transfer to Bonn main station

More information on projects involved

http://www.daad.de

CHAPTER

Project-based Workshop—7

How to Approach Global Justice?

Short Description

This Project-based Workshop invites the participants to get involved in a direct dialogue: In the framework of this workshop, participants will learn about different approaches to education for sustainable development covering different target and age groups, including persons with disabilities. All participants will have the opportunity to interact with different methods and instruments to achieve an interesting intercultural and transgenerational dialogue on global justice. An exhibition presenting the different methods and instruments accompanies this Project-based Workshop.

Workshop Schedule

1615	Arrival and welcome
1630	Split-up into learning stations
1700	Parallel learning stations with discussion groups:

1. Ecological footprint
2. Chat of the Worlds
3. World Breakfast
4. Education meets development
5. Disability and development cooperation

Participants have the possibility to rotate between stations every 15 minutes

1830	Summary and discussion
1900	Informal get-together and dinner
2000	Bus transfer to Bonn main station

More information on projects involved

http://www.inwent.org
http://www.gtz.de
http://www.bezev.de
http://www.bildung-trifft-entwicklung.de/
http://www.welthungerhilfe.de

CHAPTER

Project-based Workshop—8 ESD and ICT *Multimedia Learning*

Short Description

Multimedia and learning with ICT is becoming more and more important day-by-day. In this Project-based Workshop, different models of learning through multimedia for ESD will be introduced. A brief introduction will present the different models of ICT-based learning. Participants will then have the possibility to have hands-on experience at the different projects within a large exhibition together with representatives of projects. After this, a discussion on the process of learning through multimedia in different countries will be held.

Workshop Schedule

1630	Arrival and welcome by head of academy, F. Vogelsang and project representatives
1700	Introduction of workshops
1720	Split-up into working groups, interactive work on the themes:

	1. learning laboratory: water
	2. learning islands: a gulp of water
1830	Summary and discussion
1900	Informal get-together and dinner at academy canteen
2000	Bus transfer to Bonn main station

More information on projects involved:

http://www.creta.de;
http://www.modellversuche.bildung-lsa.de/transfer21/index.htm

Project-based Workshop—9

Non-formal Education for Sustainable Development through Experiential Learning

Short Description

Finkens Garden is an eco-social natural garden of 50,000 m^2 where pre-school and primary school children can experience nature with hands-on experiences and senses. Within the Project-based Workshop, there will be a guided tour through the project area as well as the presentation of four partner projects from the city of Aalen, Aalen University, the BUND-Centre Heilbronn and the Society for Environmental Education Baden-Würt-temberg. Participants will discuss the orientation of ESD towards experience and how to foster the interest of people of all ages for environmental topics by means of experimental learning, e.g. sowing, planting and harvesting as well as sensory experiences such as seeing, hearing, smelling, tasting and feeling; also in contact to natural elements like air, soil and water—by actively discovering and taking action.

Workshop Schedule

1630	Arrival, walk through the garden area and welcome at workshop venue
1700	Introduction to projects involved and working groups
1720	Split-up into working groups, interactive work on the themes: 1. experience sustainable events 2. global learning in the 'world garden' 3. actively discovering and understanding nature by senses 4. action-orientated energy-saving 5. experiments in pre-schools
1830	World Cafe on working group themes, including dinner
2000	Bus transfer to Bonn main station

More information on projects involved

http://www.stadt-koeln.de/6/gruen/finkens-garten
http://wwwbund.de
http://www.aalen.de
http://beratung.bildung-rp.de/
http://umweltbildung.forumieren.de/

Project-based Workshop—10
Non-formal Education for Sustainable Development in Visitor Centres, Exhibitions and Nature Experience Activities

Short Description

This Project-based Workshop focuses on non-formal learning. Three stations will deal with ESD at exhibitions and nature experience activities. The International Wadden Sea School is an educational programme for school classes from the Wadden Sea countries Denmark, Germany and the Netherlands. It wants to put into effect the idea of a trans-boundary approach to the protection of the Wadden Sea with the younger generation. The Germanwatch Climate Expedition brings climate change, its impacts and solutions into the class rooms by the means of live satellite images. By viewing the Earth from space, one can compare the situation of polar ice, glaciers, lakes, rainforests and other ecosystems in former times to their actual conditions. The Project-based Workshop takes place in NaturGut Ophoven, one of the greatest points for extracurricular environmental education in the federal state of North Rhine-Westphalia. It has a big innovative exhibition on the topic of energy and a natural site with demonstration habitats of over 60,000 square meters. It works with schools, kindergartens and adults.

Workshop Schedule

1630	Arrival and welcome
1645	Split-up in two working groups: 1. non-formal learning methods of NaturGut Ophoven: guided tour through the grounds of NaturGut Ophoven 2. learning in exhibitions: museum 'city of energy'
1735	working group: non-formal education with the Germanwatch Climate Expedition
18.25	working group: non-formal education with the International Wadden Sea School
1915	Summary and discussion of working groups
1930	Informal get-together and dinner
2000	Bus transfer to Bonn main station

More information on projects involved

http://www.naturgut-ophoven.de
http://www.iwss.org
http://www.germanwatch.org

CHAPTER

Project-based Workshop—11

UNESCO Associated Schools Working towards ESD

Short Description

The German UNESCO ASPnet has 192 member schools of all types and age groups. The main topics of its work are Human Rights, Peace and Democracy Education, Intercultural Learning, Education for Sustainable Development and World Heritage Education, to name just a few. The Associated Schools use methods like open school, interdisciplinary classes, projects for different age groups and others to implement UNESCO's aims and principles in their school programmes. Three ASP Schools will take part in the Project-based Workshop in Bonn. The Schillergymnasium Miinster will present Solar Net International, an association to support intercultural exchange projects. The Comenius Kolleg Mettingen will present group activities for first year university students based on ecological projects that were the results of German-Brazilian cooperation. The Robert Wetzlar Berufskolleg is the host school and will present projects on Sustainable cooking and barrier-free tourism within the region.

Workshop Schedule

1645	Arrival and welcome by school headmaster, M. Petz and V. Horold, National Coordinator ASPNet Germany
1715	Split-up into working groups, interactive work with students 1. Sustainable cooking 2. homeland and ESD 3. Sustainable energy 4. Sustainable prawns breeding 5. Solar Net International
1830	Summaries of working groups and conculsion
1900	Informal get-together and Sustainable dinner at school canteen
2000	Bus transfer to Bonn main station

More information on projects involved

http://www.ups-schulen.de
http://rwb.bonn.de
http://www.solarnet.tv
http://www.comenius-kolleg.de/

CHAPTER

Project-based Workshop—12

Pre-conference for the Children and Youth International Conference for the Environment (Brazil 2010)

Short Description

The project '50/50—energy efficiency and renewable energy' of the Emilie Heyermann Secondary School in Bonn is part of Agenda 21 at school and an official German Project of the UN Decade. Students from Bonn and their partner schools in Budapest (Hungary) and Buchara (Uzbekistan) will set in motion working groups on the themes of climate change, energy efficiency, renewable energy, waste avoidance and prevention of violence. Workshops will take place as a Conference at School in the lead-up to the Children and Youth International Conference for the Environment to be hosted by Brazil in 2010. This conference is a pedagogical campaign that brings together both the participation and the environmental-political dimensions for education on the theme of global responsibility. Workshop participants will get involved in direct dialogue with the students discussing their ideas of projects to be started at the school.

Workshop Schedule

1645	Arrival and welcome by school headmaster, E. Hülzhörster
1700	Introduction to the Children and Youth International Conference for the Environment (Brazil 2010) by Ministry of Education Brazil Director of Environmental Education, R. Trajber
1715	Guided tour through exhibition of school activities
1730	Split-up into working groups, interactive work within student workshop groups, presentation of workshop results by students on the themes: 1. climate change and energy efficiency 2. renewable energy 3. waste avoidance 4. prevention of violence
1830	Summaries by four student representatives of working groups
1900	Informal get-together and dinner at school canteen
2000	Bus transfer to Bonn main station

More information on projects involved

http://www.spice.bonn.de
http://confint2010.mec.gov.br

Project-based Workshop—13

Education for Sustainable Development in Life and at Work

Short Description

The House of NICA is a common pilot project of the Federal Institute for Vocational Education and Training (BIBB), the Institute for Innovation and Sustainability (IRIS) and the educational institution 'Rhine-Erft Academy', financially supported by the Federal Ministry of Education and Research. Starting with programmes like 'responsible care', there is a trend in the chemical industry towards developing a corporate culture. This goal can only be achieved with the participation of the whole staff. The pilot project NICA tries to transform the more abstract business principle of sustainable development into practical work. The pilot project is divided into the following sub-projects: development and testing of modules to integrate sustainability into VET; development and testing of a model of indicators and key figures to assess sustainability; 'House of NICA'—apprentices plan and construction of a sustainable house; The sustainable educational institution. Within the Project-based Workshop, the project will be presented by vocational students.

Workshop Schedule

1630	Arrival and welcome, D. Winzier, Federal Institute for Vocational Training and R. Overmann, Rhine-Erft Academy
1645	Presentation of pilot project NICA, sustainability in vocational education and training in the chemical industry, R. Overmann and B. Bartsch
1715	Split-up into working groups, interactive work on the themes: 1. sustainability in the chemical industry 2. House of NICA 3. assessment of sustainability and transfer into TVET 4. sustainable educational institution
1830	Excursion to the chemistry park Knapsack Alternative: discussions with project team
1900	Informal get-together and dinner
2000	Bus transfer to Bonn main station

More information on projects involved

http://www.nachhaltige-berufsbildung.de/
http://www.bibb.de

CHAPTER

Project-based Workshop—14

Starting Strong *Education for Sustainable Development in Early Childhood*

Short Description

This Project-based Workshop will show that skills and competences of fundamental importance can be nurtured long before the first day at school. The approach of 'Learning to shape life' has been implemented into everyday work at several hundred kindergartens within Germany. One of these, the day nursery in Oberhonnefeld, will discuss their work on ESD in early childhood through an exchange of ideas and experiences with participants. The implementation of this approach through information, cooperation, education, support and creativity within the federal State of Rhineland-Palatinate will be shown as well.

Workshop Schedule

1630 Arrival and welcome by P. Schnell, head of the kindergarten, and with the musical 'dance of the planets' sung by children

1700	Split-up into learning stations with interactive discussion groups on the themes: • wind • water • weather • stones • senses • wood • native Americans • fire Participants have the possibility to rotate between stations freely, dinner is included here
19.00	Summary and discussion
20.00	Bus transfer to Bonn main station

More information on projects involved

http://www.umdenken.de
http://www.lbv.de/umweltbildung/leben-gestalten-lernen.html

Index

I

J

K

L

M